FESTIVE CUISINE

*T*his book would not have been possible
without the invaluable advice and assistance
of my sister, Voula Georgitziki. I dedicate
this book to her with all my love.

Vefa Alexiadou is the leading cooking authority in Greece. A gifted cook who comes from a long line of gifted cooks, she has modernized Greek cooking using contemporary methods and equipment while retaining authentic flavor. A graduate of the University of Thessaloniki in chemistry, she also took classes in nutrition at the University of California at Berkeley. Her love of cooking motivated her to visit many foreign countries and to study culinary arts, food styling, table decoration and nutrition. Her background in chemistry has enabled her to successfully combine scientific know-how with her culinary talent. As a regular on Greece's most popular morning TV show, she continues to pass on the heritage of traditional Greek cookery to hundreds of thousands of Greek women. Vefa Alexiadou's articles and recipes appear in all the major Greek women's magazines as well as newspapers and other publications. She is the author, stylist, and publisher of her own best-selling cookbooks: "Invitation to Dinner", "Invitation to Cocktails", "Invitation to Tea", "Invitation to a Childrens Party", "Greek Cuisine", and "Greek Pastries and Desserts". Vefa Alexiadou is a member of the board of directors of ARCHESTRATOS, Center for the Preservation and Advancement of Traditional Greek Gastronomy. She was born in Volos, Greece and is married to Constantine Alexiadis, Professor at the Aristotelian University of Thessaloniki. They divide their time between their home in Thessaloniki and Athens where their two married daughters, Angela and Alexia, live.

VEFA ALEXIADOU

FESTIVE CUISINE

200 recipes, to prepare
19 festive menus

AUTHOR
VEFA K. ALEXIADOU

ART DIRECTION
KOSTIS N. KOLIOS

PHOTOGRAPHY
ZACHARIAS K. ANASTASIADIS

VEFA ALEXIADOU

EDITION

CONTENTS   PAGE

MY SINCERE THANKS

To the Kosta Boda Studio, Thessaloniki, for providing the china and silverware used for the table settings throughout the book.

To my sister, Voula Georgitzikis, for her valuable contributions to this book and for allowing the photographs in "Golden Anniversary" and "Reunion Dinner" to be taken in her home.

To my niece, Elena Georgiziki-Talli for allowing her home to be the setting for the photographs in "Festive Holiday Gathering", "Carnival Buffet", and "Happy Birthday, Grandma".

To my dear friend, Freda Matalon, for her assistance in preparing several of the dishes.

To my American friend, Linda Makris, for her assistance in the translation and editing of the English edition.

To all those who assisted in the publication of this book.

And finally, I want to thank my husband for his constructive criticism, constant support, and his invaluable assistance throughout the various stages of the publication of this book.

Vefa Alexiadou

1996 First Edition
Editor and Publisher: Vefa Alexiadou, Thessaloniki

Art Direction: Kostis Kolios, Athens
Photography: Zacharias Anastasiadis, Thessaloniki
Food Preparation: Voula Georgitziki, Thessaloniki
Food Presentation and Styling: Vefa Alexiadou
Assistant Editors: Angela & Alexia Alexiadou, Athens
Translation and Editing: Linda F. Makris, Athens
Typesetting: COM.AD, Athens
Layout: Evi Lambrou, Athens
Color Separation: Adam Hellenic Reproduction, ABEE, Athens
Montage: Andreas Androulakis, Athens
Printing: Pergamos ABEE, Athens
Binding: Kostas Papadakis, Athens

ISBN 960-90137-0-8
Copyright © Vefa Alexiadou
Leonidou 4, Metamorphosis, Athens
Tel/Fax 01/2848086

Prologue

When speaking of culture and civilization, we usually refer to sculpture, literature, poetry, music, the theater, customs and traditions. Seldom, if ever, is gastronomy listed among the arts. Perhaps it is the common aura which surrounds the subject of food and nutrition that diminishes its importance. But flavor and taste preferences, the manner in which food is served and the table is set reveal not only the traditions of a family, but also the culture of a society. This is something Vefa Alexiadou has ably demonstrated in her latest book, *Festive Cuisine,* which brilliantly blends the senses of taste, smell, and sight into a coherent, aesthetic whole. Seventh in a series of cookbooks published in Greek, the third to be published in English, *Festive Cuisine* is the culmination of her life-long experience with the culinary arts. This book will prove to be a boon not only to novice homemakers, but also will assist the more experienced who wish to improve and refine their skills and knowledge of culinary traditions. *Festive Cuisine* is a virtual treasure trove of menus and recipes accompanied by ideas for elegant presentation

and distinctive table settings for every occasion. The suggestions set forth in this priceless guide are sure to lend quality to those special moments we choose to celebrate in our lives. Leafing through this book brings to mind a quote by the American writer, Bertha Mae Smart Grosvenor, who said that cooking is an act of love. If you put all your love, energy and imagination into what you cook, the food is not only transformed into energy for blood and cells, but also it becomes a source of love and inspiration to those who eat it. And in *Festive Cuisine*, Vefa Alexiadou shows us not only how to cook, but also how to love!

Simoyi kafiri

EDITORIAL DIRECTOR OF PRACTICAL WOMAN MAGAZINE AND GENERAL SECRETARY OF "ARCESTRATOS" (CENTER FOR THE PRESERVATION & ADVANCEMENT OF TRADITIONAL GREEK GASTRONOMY)

ɪNTRODUCTION

My Dear Friends,

There are significant times and important events in our lives we wish to share with others. Such occasions call for celebration in the company of friends or family with singing and laughter, the merry clink of glasses, the exchange of gifts, and flowers. Such joyous moments become even more meaningful when we entertain in the warm, friendly atmosphere of our home. A brightly lit house full of flowers and a table graciously laid with our best linen, china, crystal and tableware provide the perfect setting for serving a tasty meal, carefully prepared and presented, accompanied by an excellent wine. This picture is completed by the presence of our loved ones to share our happiness. However charming all this may appear, successful entertaining does not just happen by chance. A certain amount of thought and effort need to be given. With proper organization and advance planning, the troublesome aspects of the preparations are reduced to a minimum.

Whether you are planning a formal dinner or simply inviting a few friends to share a meal, the suggestions in *Festive Cuisine* have been designed not only to make your job easier and more enjoyable, but also to assure the success of the occasion and the pleasure of your guests.

Vefa Alexiadou

FESTIVE CUISINE AND ENTERTAINING

Entertaining at home can and should to be fun for us as well. We want our parties to be successful, unforgettable events. *Festive Cuisine*, your personal advisor, will guide you from the planning stage to the final touches of your party, leaving time to enjoy yourself as much as your friends. The information in this book has been organized not only to guide you but also to inspire you.
The nineteen festive menus are divided into two groups: one group includes the major annual holidays such as Christmas, Easter, Carnival, Mother's Day and Father's Day, while the other group includes more personal special occasions such as engagements, weddings, baptisms, graduations, promotions, and simple friendly get-togethers. Each section includes practical information for the preparation of the recipes what wine to serve, decorations, table settings and tips for managing your time. Most recipes are designed for six persons but can easily be increased for larger numbers. The menus have been chosen not only with particular holidays in mind, but also for other festive occasions throughout the year. Many recipes are so enjoyable and easy to prepare that you will want to add them to your regular culinary repertoire. Prepare the more difficult ones when you have time, freeze, and serve any time you want to add a festive touch to your everyday fare.

ORGANIZATION AND INVITATIONS

When you decide to give a party, begin with proper organization. First select a suitable menu for the occasion, one that inspires you and is easily prepared. By inviting people who enjoy each other's company, taking into account their personalities and their interests or professions, you will create a lively atmosphere. Be sure to invite your guests well in advance, so the majority will be able to attend. For an informal gathering, phone, fax or E-mail your friends about a week before. A more formal occasion requires a printed or handwritten invitation sent one month ahead and, if numbers are a consideration, ask to be notified of non-attendance. Make arrangements if additional help is needed, especially when planning a large party. There are offices which specialize in providing trained waiters, bartenders, or other staff who will share the work or do all of it. Prepare a list of things to be done and post it in the kitchen (the fridge is a good place) where you can easily consult it. The dishes you choose to serve should be determined by the occasion. Be sure to include special ingredients and traditional foods associated with certain holidays. Remember that a few well-cooked dishes are preferable to many poorly prepared ones. Your guests should leave your table comfortably satisfied by the food and wine, not overwhelmed by an excess of it. If possible, cook and have your family sample at least a few of the recipes beforehand. This will give you more confidence in preparing them for your party. Finally, if something goes wrong at the last minute, don't panic. No one will notice the difference unless YOU draw their attention to it! This is probably the most important thing an aspiring host or hostess should remember.

THE SELECTION AND SERVING OF WINE

After choosing your menu, you should select a suitable wine. Although many wine dealers will be able to assist you

in your choice, it is a good idea to know something about the kinds of wine which compliment the foods you plan to serve. The old rule of thumb was to serve red wines with meats and white wines with fish. Today, this rule has been relaxed. Thus, poultry, white meats such as veal, and oily fish like salmon are equally compatible with a light red wine as they are with a full-bodied white wine. Sauces and garnishes will also influence your choice. If you are serving food with a rich or spicy

sauce, a dry, full-bodied aromatic wine is appropriate. On the other hand, a light cuisine calls for a delicate wine with a light bouquet. The flavors of foods and wines should never clash nor overwhelm each other; one should compliment the other. Another precept to have in mind is that white wine is always served at the beginning of the meal at 46-50°F (8-10°C) with the appetizers, the first course, salads, fish, and main courses of fish, seafood, and poultry. The same foods can also be served with a dry rosé chilled to 45-52°F (8-10°C). When the menu calls for a red wine to accompany red meat or game, it should be served (after the white wine course) at room temperature 64-72°F (18-22°C). Since the room temperature of today's homes ranges between 68°F and 75°F (20-24°C), red wine should be kept in a cool place until served. Medium sweet wines go well with fruit and most desserts. Sweet red wine is also good with fruit or can be used as an apéritif. Like other white wines, champagne is always served well chilled. Although you may want to serve the wines recommended in this book with each menu, you should depend more on your own personal preference and that of your guests. Above all, choose a good quality wine. It is better to serve a modest amount of good wine than a lot of mediocre vintage. The ideal wineglass is one which allows the color, clarity and bouquet of the wine to be savored. This is why wine is usually served in transparent tulip-shaped stemware of fine crystal or glass. Open the bottle by removing the top of the capsule and the cork but leave intact the part of the capsule below the neck-ring, as proof of its

quality. When serving wine, always hold the bottle by its body, never by its neck. Pour the wine from just above the glass, not allowing the neck of the bottle to rest on the rim. Fill the glass only to the middle, allowing room for the wine to be swirled and the bouquet to be inhaled before the wine is sipped. The appropriate wine contributes unbelievable enjoyment to a meal.

SHOPPING

Carefully read the recipes and make your shopping list about a month before your party. Check the list and delete ingredients you have on hand in your pantry. First buy the ingredients needed for the dishes you can prepare ahead of time. Make a separate list for candles, flowers, and decorations as well as other serving pieces, utensils or equipment.

CREATING ATMOSPHERE

Low lighting and the flicker of candles will help create the right

atmosphere. Select good quality non-drip candles of real wax, avoiding the aromatic ones. Music is an absolute must but it should be kept in the background to allow for an easy flow of conversation. Pay careful attention to the table setting. You can create a pleasant and festive atmosphere for your guests by decorating your table with the appropriate accessories for the season or occasion, arranged with your personal touch and in keeping with the theme of your party. Begin by using your best table linens, either a well-ironed tablecloth or attractive place mats at each place. A lace tablecloth looks even more spectacular over a solid-color lining which can be coordinated with the colors in your china, napkins, flowers, candles and other decorations. Flowers in vases of various sizes placed in every corner of your home lend the perfect festive touch. The most important decoration on your table is a centerpiece of fresh or dried flowers arranged in a low oblong base, with or without candles. In keeping with your theme or the season, you may use shells, fruits or vegetables to express your distinctive style

and imagination. An ambience of style, harmony and grace is sure to set the scene for a spectacular dining experience your guests won't soon forget.

NAPKINS

One particularly charming yet necessary dining accessory is the beautifully folded napkin. The tradition of decoratively folded napkins began at the court of Henry the Third and rapidly became popular beyond the borders of France. In order to successfully fold a napkin, you must have a steam iron and spray starch to keep the fabric the way you have folded it. A rosebud or other flower blossom placed in the fold of the napkin will lend a note of freshness to your table. The designs shown in the various table settings are described in detail with sketches at the end of the book. Always fold the napkins before the day of the party. If you try to do this job the same day, it is certain that in the rush of last minute preparations, you will not have sufficient time to fold them properly.

TABLEWARE AND PLACE SETTINGS

In the past there were certain time-honored rules which strictly governed all aspects of the arrangement of china, silver and crystal on a table. Dining, as entertainment, was very much a formal affair. The simplification of modern life has, however, caused a dramatic relaxation of the old rules. It is no longer considered a serious breach of etiquette if special service for the fish course is not set. Most of these special utensils are no longer included in modern sets of tableware. The placement

and number of plates, glasses and silverware should, however, be guided by the nature of the foods and the order in which they are to be served as well as the practicality of how they will be eaten. Thus, the dinner plate should be placed first, with a smaller plate on top for the first course. If soup is being served, a bowl should be placed on top of that. Service plates and hot pads not only serve the purpose of protecting the table top, but they also add color and decor to your table setting. Place the knives to the right of the plates with the cutting

edge toward the plate. Forks are placed to the left, the smaller salad fork on the outside and the larger fork for the main course next to the plate. Soupspoons are set to the right of the knives and if you are serving pasta for the first course, place a spoon in the place of the first knife. Dessert forks, teaspoons and cheese knives are set above the plate, with the handle of the spoon and knife to the right and that of the fork to the left. The salad plate is placed above the forks with the butter plate to the left of the forks. The water glass should be placed above the tip of the larger knife and the wine glass to its right. Napkins can be set either on the plates, in one of the glasses, under the forks or to the left of the forks. Remember, these suggestions have been given as a general guide, and the creation of a comfortable, pleasant table setting is entirely a personal matter.

WHAT TO SERVE

When your guests first arrive, welcome them with a before-dinner drink (apéritif) and a light appetizer. Choose one or prepare both of the suggestions given with each menu. Remember that an appetizer is meant to whet the appetite, not spoil it. The appetizer or the first course can be replaced with a hot or cold soup served at the table. Serve the first course when all the guests have been seated and don't start removing the plates before everyone has finished. After the tableware from the first course has been cleared away, bring the main course to the table with the garnishes, gravy boat and the salad. The bread may be placed on the butter plates before the guests sit down. Extra bread can be served in a basket

lined with a clean napkin. Again, do not remove soiled plates before everyone has finished the main course. If cheese and fruit are included in the menu, serve them at the end of the meal after clearing the table and setting out clean plates. Clear away the used glasses and leave those for the wine or champagne being served with the fruit, cheese and dessert. The dessert course may be served in the living room with coffee and liqueur, or whatever your guests prefer.

THE FRUIT

Fresh fruit of the season is an ideal way to end a meal, especially a heavy one. Serve the fruit in decorated bowls;

if you have the time and the artistic talent, be creative and serve the fruit in a large hollowed out melon or pumpkin. Take your inspiration from their size and shape, transforming them into baskets, boats, swans or whatever your imagination brings to mind.

THE CHEESES

An appetizing platter of natural cheeses attractively garnished is a fitting end to any good meal. Fresh fruits, especially grapes, not only decorate your cheese platter, but also combine well with the taste of most cheeses. You can take your inspiration from the various cheese platters shown in this book or make your own combinations according to your personal taste and the variety of cheeses available. Taking advantage of the theme of your party, add a festive note to your table by decorating the cheeses as we have done in *Festive Holiday Gathering, Valentine's Dinner*, and *Wedding Reception*. Cheese should always be served with bread sticks, crackers, or melba toast. The cheese course extends the pleasant mood at your table by giving your guests the opportunity to savor their wine and the lively conversation.

BASIC RECIPES

In this section, recipes for some basic ingredients are given. Although available commercially, when made at home, they make a big difference. When you have time, for example,

you can prepare meat, fish or chicken stock to keep on hand in your freezer. Also you can make mayonnaise and keep it in the refrigerator. With meat stock as a base, you can prepare a light tasty consommé instead of the appetizer or first course.

MEAT STOCK

2 lbs (1 kg) beef or veal knuckle bones
2 lbs (1 kg) meat trimmings (neck, shank or ribs)
12 cups (3 l) water
2 medium onions
4 large carrots
1 small stalk of celery
1 leek
1 head of garlic
4-5 sprigs of parsley
2 cloves stuck into one of the onions
1 bay leaf
salt

Put the meat and bones into a large, heavy-bottomed soup pot and add cold water to cover. Slowly bring to a boil over medium heat and skim off the scum which rises to the top. Keep skimming, occasionally adding some cold water to slow the boiling, until no more scum forms. Add all the other ingredients and continue skimming until the boiling point is reached. Reduce heat and simmer slowly for 5-7 hours, occasionally skimming off the scum and excess fat from the surface. Strain through a fine sieve and discard solids. Allow stock to cool, skim fat from the surface, or refrigerate the stock and lift off the solidified fat. Divide the jellied stock in 1 or 2-cup portions in heavy plastic bags or containers. Stock will keep up to 1 week in refrigerator and 6 months in a freezer.
Yield: 8 cups of stock.

CHICKEN STOCK

Follow the procedure for the meat stock. Substitute chicken wings, backs and necks for the meat. For variety, combine chicken and meat bones. After cutting up meat or chicken for cooking, the uncooked meat bones and chicken necks, wings and backs can be frozen. When you have enough, make the stock and freeze. This way you will always have delicious homemade stock on hand for rice pilaf or any other recipe.

FISH STOCK (FUMET)

1 lb (½ kg) sole or other flat fish bones (excluding fins & tails)
1 onion, sliced
1 celery stalk, chopped
1 carrot, thinly sliced
1 leek, sliced
1 garlic clove (optional)
4 cups (1 l) tap water
1 cup white wine
1 tablespoon lemon juice
6 parsley sprigs
1 bay leaf
6 peppercorns

Rinse fish bones and put in a pot with the onion, celery, carrot, leek, garlic and a little salt. Add the water and bring slowly to a boil. Skim off the scum that rises to the top. Keep skimming, until the broth reaches the boiling point. Add the remaining ingredients, cover, and simmer for about 40 minutes. Strain the stock through a fine sieve lined with cheesecloth and discard the solids. Cool slightly, and then refrigerate until jelled. Divide into 4 parts, put in plastic bags or containers, and freeze. Stock will keep up to 3 days in the refrigerator and

2 months in the freezer.
Yield: 4 cups of stock.

MAYONNAISE

2 eggs
1 teaspoon prepared mustard
1/8 teaspoon sugar
1/3 cup lemon juice
1 teaspoon salt
1/4 teaspoon black pepper
1/4 teaspoon cayenne pepper or paprika
2 cups safflower or corn oil

Put all the ingredients except for the oil in a food processor. Blend for a few seconds at medium speed. With the processor on, pour the oil through the opening in a thin steady stream. Turn off as soon as all the oil has been added.
Yield: 2½ cups.

VEGETABLE CONSOMMÉ

8 cups meat stock
1/4 cup julienned carrots
1/4 cup julienned radishes
1/4 cup julienned leeks
1/4 cup tender parsley stems
salt and pepper
croutons

Steam the vegetables in 1 cup of water until crisp-tender. Drain and stir into the meat stock. Heat it just to the boiling point and season with salt and freshly ground black pepper. Serve the consommé hot with croutons.
A consommé should be clear. If it is cloudy, clarify it before adding the vegetables as follows: Whip two egg whites to a soft meringue and add to the stock. Stir over medium heat just to the boiling point. Remove from the heat and allow to cool 10 minutes. Strain through a sieve lined with paper towels.

VALENTINE'S DINNER

MENU

Feta Cheese Appetizer

Valentine Pizza

Stuffed Beef-Patties
Potatoes with Mozzarella and Bacon

Lovers' Bread

Gift-Wrapped Cake

Melon Basket

Cabernet Sauvignon or Champagne

add the milk. Then mix in the eggs, grated Parmesan, salt and pepper. If the mixture is too stiff, add a little more milk. Butter a 2-quart ovenproof (18x24cm) dish and sprinkle with breadcrumbs. Spread half the potato mixture in it and sprinkle with the bacon pieces and grated mozzarella. Pipe the remaining potato mixture on top, using a pastry bag fitted with a large star tip. Brush the surface with the egg white. Bake in a medium 350°F (180°C) oven for 35 minutes or until the top is browned. Serve hot.

Preparation time 1 hour and 30 minutes

Feta Cheese Appetizer

1	lb (500 gr) mild feta cheese
1	hot green pepper
4	tablespoons olive oil
1	tablespoon vinegar
1/4	teaspoon black pepper
1	large canned pimento
1	large green bell pepper

Cut cheese into 2-3 pieces and soak in water for 10 minutes. Meanwhile, saute the hot green pepper in the oil or roast under the broiler. Peel and remove seeds. Mash or grate the cheese and put in a food processor with the hot pepper, vinegar, and freshly ground black pepper. Process while gradually adding the oil in which the green pepper was sauteed or 4 tablespoons fresh olive oil. Continue blending until smooth. Refrigerate until firm. Shape into a ball. Using large and small heart-shaped cutters, cut "valentines" from the pimento. From the green pepper, cut the two parts of the arrow. Place them on the cheese ball, cover with plastic wrap, and refrigerate until ready to serve.

Preparation time
30 minutes

Potatoes with Mozzarella and Bacon

2	lbs (1 kg) potatoes
2	tablespoons butter
1/2	cup milk
2	eggs, slightly beaten
1/4	cup grated Parmesan or kefalotiri cheese
	salt and pepper, to taste
2	cups (200 gr) grated mozzarella cheese
8	oz (250 gr) bacon, chopped
2	tablespoons dry bread crumbs
1	egg white, slightly beaten

Wash and peel the potatoes; cut into quarters. Simmer with a small amount of water until soft and the water has been absorbed. Pass through a food mill or puree in a food processor. Stir in the butter and gradually

Valentine Pizza

The Dough
3   cups all purpose flour
1   teaspoon dry yeast
1/2 teaspoon salt
1   cup water
1   tablespoon corn oil

The Filling
2   cups (200 gr) shredded mozzarella cheese
7   oz (200 gr) bacon, chopped
3- 4 oz (100 gr) mushrooms, sliced
3   tablespoons olive oil
1/4 cup barbeque sauce
1   small green bell pepper, finely chopped
1   large tomato, thinly sliced
     black pepper, to taste
1   tablespoon finely chopped fresh basil
1   cup grated provolone cheese
2   hearts cut from canned pimento for garnish
1   sprig fresh basil for garnish

Mix all the dough ingredients in the bowl of an electric mixer fitted with a dough hook. Beat until dough gathers around the hook and continue beating for about 5 minutes at low speed. Oil a 12-inch (30-cm) heart-shaped pan. Spread dough evenly into it using the palms of your hands. Brush with 1 tablespoon oil and sprinkle with mozzarella. Scatter the bacon over the cheese. Saute the mushrooms in the remaining olive oil. When they are wilted, add the barbecue sauce and simmer over low heat until liquid is absorbed. Spread the mushroom sauce over the bacon and arrange the tomatoes on top. Scatter the chopped pepper and basil over the entire surface and sprinkle generously with black pepper. Finally, sprinkle the grated provolone on top. At this stage the pizza may be frozen. Bake pizza in a 200°C (400°F) oven for 35 minutes. Serve hot, garnished with a sprig of fresh basil and two red pepper hearts.

Preparation time 1 hour

Stuffed Beef-Patties

1   lb (450 gr) ground beef
1/3   cup grated onion
2   tablespoons olive oil
1/2   teaspoon thyme
1/2   teaspoon ground coriander
2   teaspoons dry bread crumbs
       salt and pepper, to taste
1/3   cup beef stock
2   strips of bacon, chopped
1/3   cup coarsely shredded mozzarella cheese
2   tablespoons heavy cream

The Sauce
1/4   cup olive oil
1/2   cup sliced mushrooms
2   tablespoons minced onion

1/2   clove garlic, mashed
1   cup fresh or canned tomatoes, crushed and
       pressed through a sieve
1-2   tablespoons chili sauce
2   fresh leaves of basil
       salt and pepper, to taste
       whole and chopped fresh basil leaves for garnish

In a large bowl, mix ground beef with the onion, oil, herbs, bread crumbs, salt and pepper. Knead mixture, adding as much stock as necessary for it to be light and hold its shape. Cover and refrigerate for 1 hour. Meanwhile, in a small bowl mix the bacon with the mozzarella and cream. To make the sauce, heat the oil and saute the mushrooms. Remove from pan with a slotted spoon. In the same oil, lightly saute the onion and the garlic. Add the remaining ingredients, cover, and simmer over low heat until thick. Remove the basil and strain for a smooth shiny sauce. Stir in the mushrooms, if desired; otherwise, serve separately. Knead the meat mixture a little more; if it is too stiff, add a little more stock. Divide into 4 parts and shape into 3-inch (8-cm) round patties. Spread the mozzarella mixture evenly on two patties and cover them with the remaining two. Form into heart-shapes, brush with oil, and grill on charcoal or under the broiler for 15 minutes, turning twice. Serve hot accompanied by the sauce and mushrooms; garnish with the basil.

Preparation time 1 hour and 15 minutes

Lovers' Bread

3	cups bread flour
3	tablespoons sugar
1	tablespoon dry yeast
1½	cups warm water 100°F (40°C)
1/2	cup grated Parmesan cheese
1	tablespoon coarsely ground black pepper
1	teaspoon salt
2	tablespoons olive oil
1	egg yolk beaten with
1	teaspoon water
	sesame seeds

In a bowl, mix 1 cup of the flour with sugar and yeast. Add ²/₃ cup warm water and mix. Cover and allow to rise for about 10 minutes. In a large bowl, mix the rest of the flour, cheese, salt, and pepper. Add the yeast mixture, the oil, and enough water to make a pliable dough. Place dough on worktop and knead for 8-10 minutes, until smooth and elastic. Brush with a little oil, cover, and allow to rise in a warm place until doubled in bulk. Knead again for 2-3 minutes on a lightly floured surface. Divide into three equal parts. Roll one part, into a long ¹/₃ inch (¹/₂ cm) thick strip. Divide in two and cut out two "arrows". Roll the other two parts of dough into two long oval loaves. Cover and allow to rise for 10 minutes. With a sharp knife cut lengthwise into the center of the loaf without cutting through completely, allowing an 1 inch (2-cm) closed space at each end. Pull sides apart forming a circle. Lift the top end and pull down into the circle forming the top of the "heart". Form the bottom tip of the "heart" accordingly. Place the hearts and arrows on a large greased baking sheet, cover, and allow to rise another 15 minutes. Brush with egg yolk and sprinkle generously with sesame seeds. Bake in a 400°F (200°C) oven for about 15 minutes. Remove from the oven and cool. It may be frozen until ready to use.

Preparation time 2 hours and 30 minutes

Gift-Wrapped Cake

The Cake
4   eggs
2/3   cup sugar
2/3   cup self-rising flour
1/3   cup cornstarch
1   teaspoon vanilla extract
6   tablespoons Grand Marnier

The Filling
2   cups whipping cream
5-6   oz (150 gr) semi-sweet baking chocolate or chips
1/2   teaspoon vanilla extract
5-6   oz (150 gr) semi-sweet white chocolate or chips
1/2   teaspoon vanilla extract

The 7- Minute Frosting
2   egg whites
1½   cups powdered sugar
1/4   teaspoon cream of tartar
1/4   teaspoon salt
1/3   cup water
1   teaspoon vanilla extract

The Garnish

1/3   recipe almond paste (page 184)
     pink, yellow & green food coloring

The Cake: Beat the eggs and sugar with a mixer at high speed until light and thick, about 15 minutes; add the flavorings. Sift the flour with the cornstarch. Sift again into the beaten eggs, a little at a time, and gently fold in. Pour the batter into a buttered rectangular cake pan, 7x10 inches (18x25 cm). Bake the cake in a 350 °F (180 °C) oven for 30-35 minutes. Cool and divide into three layers.

The Filling: Place half the whipping cream in a small saucepan and heat until it just begins to simmer. Remove from heat, add the dark chocolate, ¹/₂ teaspoon vanilla, and beat until smooth. Cool and refrigerate until it starts to thicken. Beat with a wire whisk until thick. Repeat with the other half of the cream, the white chocolate and ¹/₂ teaspoon vanilla. Put the fillings in separate pastry bags fitted with plain wide tips. Refrigerate until ready to use.

The Frosting: Place the ingredients in a double boiler over low heat and beat with the mixer at high speed for 7 minutes, until frosting thickens and holds stiff peaks.

To Decorate the Cake: Place the first cake layer on a platter and sprinkle with 2 tablespoons Grand Marnier. With the pastry bags, pipe alternate ribbons of the white and dark chocolate fillings lengthwise on the cake layer, completely covering the surface. Place the second cake layer on top, sprinkle with 2 tablespoons Grand Marnier, and repeat the procedure with the other half of the filling. Cover with the third cake layer and sprinkle with the last 2 tablespoons of liqueur. Cover the top and sides of cake with the 7-minute frosting, smoothing the surface with a spatula.

To Garnish: Prepare the almond paste as in the recipe "Bonnet de Nuit"(page 184) or buy ready-made paste. Color half the paste pink; divide the rest in two parts and color one part yellow, the other part green. Roll out the paste into a long narrow strip and with a scallop-edged wheel, cut narrow ribbons into three parts, two for the length and width of the cake and the rest for the bow. From the yellow and green pastes, form one rose and two leaves as in the recipe "Box of Roses Torte"(page 72). Place the ribbons, rose, and leaves on the cake and you will have a cake that truly resembles a gift-wrapped package.

Preparation time depends on your dexterity

Melon Basket

Choose a perfect round winter melon. With a sharp knife, outline a zigzag around the circumference slightly above the middle of the melon. Along this outline, cut the melon in half. Be sure that the top is smaller than the bottom half. Scoop out the seeds. Using your imagination, arrange various seasonal fruits in the bottom half and cover with the top. Refrigerate until ready to serve.

With a toothpick, stick a large red bow at the side before presenting it to your loved one and watch his/her face light up at its contents.

Preparation time 30 minutes

Organizing your Valentine Dinner

A simple, youthful and very impressive menu which every working man or woman can easily prepare to serve his/her loved one for Valentine's Day.
❀ *Each recipe serves 2 persons.*
❀ *Well in advance, prepare the beef patties, pizza, bread and the dessert. Store them in the freezer.*
❀ *Three days in advance, prepare the cheese appetizer without the garnish and refrigerate.*
❀ *The day before, prepare the potatoes, the melon basket with the fruits, and refrigerate.*
❀ *The evening before, set the table down to the last special detail and garnish the cheese appetizer with the hearts.*
❀ *In the morning before leaving for work, remove items from the freezer. And don't forget the gift. He or she will bring the roses.*
❀ *One hour before, put the champagne on ice and bake the pizza.*
❀ *While eating the pizza, grill the beef patties and heat the potatoes in the microwave. Bon Appétit.*

EVENING BY THE FIRE

MENU

Chicken Liver Pâté or
Cheese with Basil Appetizer

❧

Zucchini-Stuffed Crepes

❧

Beef Bourguignon or Stroganoff
Molded Risotto Ring

❧

Carrot Salad in Bibb Lettuce

❧

Bagels

❧

Praline Torte or
Caramel Candy Baskets

❧

Rosé and Dry Red Wine

Chicken Liver Pâté

1   lb (450 gr) chicken livers
1/2   cup butter
1   large onion, grated
1/2   teaspoon thyme
1   bay leaf, broken into small pieces
6   strips of bacon, chopped
3-4   oz (100 gr) mushrooms, thinly sliced
1/2   cup whipping cream
3   tablespoons sherry
2   tablespoons brandy
1/4   teaspoon powdered ginger
       salt and pepper, to taste
2   whole bay leaves for garnish
1/4   cup unsalted clarified butter, melted

Soak the livers in lightly salted water for 1 hour. Meanwhile, heat the butter and add the onion, thyme, bay leaf, bacon, and the mushrooms. Saute until wilted, taking care not to brown. Strain the livers, rinse, and remove the membranes and veins. Add to the pan with sauteed ingredients. Cover and simmer for about 10 minutes, until the livers and mushrooms are soft. Add the cream, sherry, brandy, ginger, salt, and pepper. Mix well and simmer over low heat until the mixture thickens.Cool slightly and blend in a food processor, until smooth. Press the mixture through a fine sieve. Put liver pâté in a small soufflé dish and garnish with two whole bay leaves. Cover with the melted butter and refrigerate. The butter will keep the pâté from drying out and spoiling. Will keep for several weeks in the refrigerator. Serve with small crackers.

Preparation time 2 hours

Cheese with Basil Appetizer

1/2   cup pine nuts
4   cups fresh basil leaves
1   small clove garlic
       salt and pepper, to taste
1/3   cup olive oil
1   lb (450 gr) ricotta, or cream cheese
1/3   cup grated Parmesan, kefalotiri, or Romano cheese
1-2   small sprigs of basil for garnish

Lightly brown the pine nuts in a frying pan over medium heat, stirring constantly. In a food processor, blend the basil, garlic, salt, pepper and 2 tablespoons pine nuts.While slowly adding the oil in a thin stream, continue processing until smooth. Set aside. Combine the ricotta with the Parmesan and beat until well blended. Add the basil mixture and continue beating until smooth and thick. Line a small round bowl with cheesecloth and press the cheese-basil mixture into it, so it takes the shape of the bowl. Cover and refrigerate overnight. When ready to serve, unmold on a plate. Remove the cheesecloth and press the remaining whole pine nuts onto the surface. Garnish with a small sprig of fresh basil. Serve with small crackers.

Preparation time 12 hours

Zucchini-Stuffed Crepes

1½   lbs (750 gr) zucchini
3   tablespoons corn oil
2/3   cup grated Romano cheese
2/3   cup grated Swiss cheese
1/3   cup finely chopped dill
     salt and pepper, to taste
2/3   cup whipping cream
15   crepes
3   extra tablespoons grated Parmesan or kefalotiri cheese

Thinly slice zucchini by hand or with a food processor. Salt lightly and drain in a colander for 1 hour. Squeeze out excess moisture by lightly pressing between palms. Heat oil in a pan, add zucchini slices and simmer until soft, stirring occasionally. Remove pan from the heat and add the remaining ingredients, salt, if necessary, freshly ground pepper, and ¼ cup of the cream. Place 2 tablespoons of zucchini filling on each crepe, prepared as in the following recipe. Freeze the remaining crepes for another use. Fold in the sides and roll up. Place in a lightly buttered ovenproof dish. Brush with remaining cream and sprinkle with grated Parmesan. At this stage they may be frozen. Bake in a 400 °F (200 °C) oven for about 45 minutes, until the tops are lightly brown. Serve hot. Alternatively, the zucchini can be replaced with leeks, white part only. Blanch and strain out excess juice before use. Replace the dill with parsley.

Preparation time 2 hours

Crepes

1   cup all purpose flour
1/8   teaspoon salt
2   eggs, slightly beaten
1   tablespoons brandy
1¼   cups milk
2   tablespoons unsalted butter, melted

In a mixing bowl, place the flour, salt, eggs, brandy, and a little of the milk. Beat at low speed until thick and smooth. Beating continuously at medium speed, gradually add the rest of the milk and the melted butter. Beat for 1 minute at high speed. Allow batter to rest for 1 hour. Strain through a sieve to remove any lumps. Prepare crepes with a special crepe-maker or in a small teflon-coated frying pan. If the batter gets too thick, thin with a little milk. Makes about 15 crepes.

Preparation time 15 minutes (using the crepe-maker)

Beef Bourguignon

3 lbs (1½ kg) fillet of beef, cut into 1 inch cubes
2 tablespoons butter
2 tablespoons olive oil
12 shallots or pearl onions, peeled and blanched
12 baby carrots (or 12 pieces of carrot), blanched
3 strips of bacon, chopped
8 oz (250 gr) fresh button mushrooms

The Sauce
4 tablespoons butter
1 clove garlic, mashed
2 tablespoons flour
1 cup dry red wine
1 cup beef stock
1 teaspoon sugar
   salt and pepper, to taste

Divide the meat in 2 or 3 portions. Heat butter and oil in a pan, and brown the portions of meat separately, on all sides. Remove with slotted spoon and set aside. In the same pan, lightly saute the onions. Remove with slotted spoon and set aside. Saute the bacon and mushrooms, stirring constantly until the mushrooms start to wilt. Set aside. In another pan, prepare the sauce. Heat the butter and lightly saute the garlic and flour. Remove from the heat and slowly add the wine and the stock; return to heat, stirring constantly, until the sauce thickens. Put the meat in an ovenproof dish and pour the sauce over it. Cover with aluminum foil and bake in a medium 350 °F (180 °C) oven for 1 hour. Add the onions, mushrooms, bacon and carrots; mix, and continue baking for 30 minutes, or until the meat is tender. Turn into a prepared phyllo basket and serve immediately.

Preparation time 1 hour and 30 minutes

Beef Stroganoff

1/4 cup flour
1/2 teaspoon salt
1/8 teaspoon black pepper
3 lbs (1½ kg) fillet of beef, cut in thin strips ½x2 inches (1x5 cm)
1 lb (500 gr) small mushrooms
1/3 cup olive oil
1 cup beef stock
1/2 cup water
3 tablespoons tomato juice
1 tablespoon Worcestershire sauce
2 teaspoons prepared mustard
1½ cups sour cream or strained yogurt

In a large plastic bag, mix the flour with the salt and pepper. Shake the pieces of meat in the bag, to coat well. Empty into a colander and shake gently, to remove excess flour. Heat the oil in a large frying pan and saute the mushrooms until wilted. Remove with slotted spoon and set aside. In the same oil, lightly saute the meat. Add the stock, water,

tomato juice, Worcestershire sauce, mustard, and mushrooms. Cover and simmer 20-30 minutes, or until meat is tender. Cool slightly. Stir in the sour cream and slowly heat to the boiling point. Turn into the phyllo basket and serve immediately.

Preparation time 1 hour and 30 minutes

Phyllo Basket

Cut 7-8 sheets of phyllo large enough to amply cover the bottom and sides of a 10-inch (25-cm) round baking pan. One by one, brush well with melted butter and lay in the pan, one on top of the other, allowing the edges to ruffle. On the bottom, place an ovenproof plate slightly smaller in diameter than the pan and bake in a hot oven, 400 °F (200 °C), for about 25 minutes. Remove the plate and continue baking for another 15 minutes, until the phyllo sheets are well-browned. Allow the basket to cool, carefully remove from the baking pan, and set on a platter.

Preparation time 1 hour

Bagels

2 teaspoons dry yeast
2 teaspoons sugar
1 cup lukewarm milk 100 °F (40 °C)
4 cups bread flour
1 teaspoon salt
3 tablespoons corn oil
1 egg white, slightly beaten
1 egg yolk beaten with
1 teaspoon water
   onion seeds

Dissolve the yeast and 1 teaspoon sugar in the lukewarm milk and let it stand until it foams. Place the flour in a large bowl and make a well in the center. Put in the remaining sugar, salt, oil, slightly beaten egg white, milk and yeast. Mix, gradually combining the flour from the sides, to form a pliable dough. Knead on a floured surface for 5 minutes and allow to rise about 1 hour. Roll the dough out, on a lightly floured surface, into a 5x7-inch (12x18-cm) rectangle and divide into 18 strips. Roll each into a thin 8-inch (20-cm) rope, wet the ends to make them stick, and form into circles. Arrange on a greased baking sheet, cover with a cloth and allow to rise in a warm place for 10 minutes. Meanwhile, bring half a large pot of water to a boil. Maintaining a constant simmer, cook a few bagels at a time, 15 seconds on each side. Remove with a slotted spoon, drain together with the spoon on paper towels, and place bagels on a buttered baking sheet. Brush with egg yolk, sprinkle with onion seeds and bake in a 400 °F (200 °C) oven for 20 minutes, until brown. Cool on a wire rack, seal in plastic bag, and freeze until ready to serve.

Preparation time 3 hours

Molded Risotto Ring

2   cups long-grain rice
1/4   cup butter
1/3   cup chopped celery
1/3   cup chopped red bell pepper
1/3   cup chopped green bell pepper
5   green onions, finely chopped
1   cup canned corn
1/4   cup finely chopped parsley

In a large pan, bring 5 cups of water to a boil. Stir in the rice and 2 teaspoons salt. Cover and simmer for 20 minutes, until all the water has been absorbed. Melt the butter in another pan, add the celery, green and red pepper, the onions, and the corn. Cook on high heat for 2 minutes, stirring constantly. Empty this mixture and the parsley into the pan containing the rice and stir lightly until well mixed. Pack the risotto into a lightly oiled 9-inch (23-cm) mold and even out with the back of a large spoon. Unmold onto a platter and serve the risotto hot. Garnish with a flower cut from the stem end of a red pepper, and two sprigs of parsley.

Preparation time 30 minutes

Carrot Salad in Bibb Lettuce

1   head of chinese cabbage or curly decorative lettuce
6   large carrots, grated
2   stalks of celery, chopped
1   bunch of radishes, thinly sliced
    several tender lettuce hearts

The Dressing
1   cup mayonnaise
3   tablespoons sour cream
1   teaspoon mild prepared mustard
1   teaspoon lemon juice
    salt and black pepper

Cut and separate 10 large leaves from the head of lettuce. Wash and drain well. Arrange around the edge of a platter. Heap the celery in the center. Fill each leaf with the grated carrots and place the radishes around the celery. Arrange the lettuce hearts attractively. Mix the dressing ingredients and place a spoonful on the carrots, or dress the salad with oil and lemon, two parts oil to one part lemon.

Preparation time 30 minutes

Caramel Candy Baskets

2   *cups sugar*
2/3   *cup water*
1/4   *teaspoon cream of tartar or*
1   *teaspoon lemon juice or vinegar*
1/8   *teaspoon beeswax (optional)*

Place all the ingredients in a small saucepan (copper is preferable). Bring the mixture to a boil over medium heat. Do not stir, just swirl the pan. Increase the heat and boil, until the liquid turns pale amber, and the temperature on a candy thermometer reaches 260 °F (130 °C). Remove from the heat and immediately set the pan in a bowl of cold water. (This will stabilize the temperature, so it does not rise anymore. Above 270 °F, spun sugar will look brassy instead of golden). If the mixture is too hot, it will fall in droplets instead of strings and will not spin. The optional wax is edible and coats the strands of spun sugar, making them easier to work with. To form the baskets, lightly butter the outside of a small metal custard cup. With one hand, hold it above the pan containing the caramel. With the other hand, dip a fork or wooden spoon into the caramel and vigorously twirl it around the outside of the metal cup, allowing the strands to fall in long, thin threads. Twirling must be continuous or too many droplets will form. Some droplets are necessary, to add extra gloss. Place the cups upside down, and allow the caramel to cool and solidify. Carefully take the caramel baskets off the custard cups and keep in an air tight container. You can serve ice cream and chocolate-covered seasonal fruits in the baskets. They may be kept in the freezer in an air tight container.

Preparation time 1 hour

Praline Torte

12   *oz (350 gr) ladyfingers*

The Praline
1½   *cups sugar*
3   *tablespoons water*
1½   *cups blanched almonds*

The Syrup
1½   *cups water*
1/2   *cup sugar*
3   *tablespoons instant coffee*
4   *tablespoons cocoa*
1   *tablespoon brandy*

The Filling
1   *cup softened unsalted butter*
1   *cup powdered sugar*
4   *egg yolks*
3   *egg whites*
1/8 *teaspoon almond extract or*
1   *teaspoon vanilla extract*

The Garnish
1   *cup whipping cream*
1-3   *tablespoons powdered sugar*
7   *After-Eight mints, cut diagonally in half*
14   *small white chocolate rolls*

Prepare the Praline: Put the sugar and water in a small saucepan and bring to a boil over medium heat. Increase the heat and boil until the liquid turns pale amber, 260 °F (130 °C) on a candy thermometer. Remove from the heat, and mix in the almonds; immediately spread the mixture on a buttered sheet of aluminum foil placed on the bottom of a large baking sheet. Allow to cool; when it is brittle, break into large pieces and crush them coarsely. Set aside in an airtight container.

Prepare the Syrup: Mix the coffee, cocoa, and sugar and dissolve in the water. Boil a few minutes forming a light syrup. Let it cool and stir in the brandy. Set aside.

Prepare the Frosting: Beat the butter with half the sugar until fluffy. Continue beating while adding, one by one, the egg yolks. In a separate bowl, beat the whites, until they form soft peaks. Beating continuously, add the remaining sugar a little at a time, until the mixture holds stiff peaks. Fold the meringue into the butter mixture with the extract of your choice.

Assemble the Torte: Place the ring from a 9-inch (22 cm) springform pan on a large round platter. Arrange 1/3 of the ladyfingers inside the ring after dipping each one briefly in the syrup. Cover with 1/3 of the filling and sprinkle with 1/3 of the praline. Repeat the same procedure two more times. Refrigerate the torte until firm. Beat the whipping cream with a little powdered sugar until stiff. Place in a pastry bag fitted with a large star tip, remove the ring, and garnish the sides of the torte. If desired, garnish with the chocolate mints and white chocolate rolls. Refrigerate until ready to serve.

Preparation time 2 hours (refrigeration time is not included)

Organizing your Evening by the Fire

An easy and tasty menu for a friendly gathering by the fire on a cold winter's evening. Serve a light rosé wine with the appetizers and the crepes and accompany the meat course with dry red wine.

❀ *Each recipe serves 6 persons.*

❀ *Well in advance, prepare the bagels, the crepes, and the caramel baskets and store them in the freezer.*

❀ *Three days in advance, prepare the liver pâté and the cheese ball. Store in the refrigerator.*

❀ *Two days in advance, prepare the praline torte and refrigerate.*

❀ *The day before, prepare the phyllo basket. Prepare all the ingredients needed for the meat dish of your choice, and the risotto.*

❀ *The evening before, set the table.*

❀ *In the morning, remove the bagels and the crepes from the freezer. Prepare the salad and refrigerate. Dress it just before serving.*

❀ *During the day, prepare the meat dish and the risotto.*

❀ *After this hearty winter supper, refresh your guests by serving them ice cream in the caramel baskets garnished with maraschino cherries dipped in chocolate.*

CARNIVAL BUFFET

MENU

Smoked Salmon or
Cheese and Eggplant Croquettes

Seafood Parcels

Miniature Stuffed Tomatoes and
Peppers

Risotto with Squid

Carnival Cheese Platter

Carnival Salad Bar

Ice Cream Tartlets or
Cannoli ala Siciliana

Pumpkin Basket with Fresh Fruit

Rosé or Dry White Wine

Cheese and Eggplant Croquettes

8   large eggplants
1/2   cup dry bread crumbs
1/4   cup grated Parmesan or mild kefalotiri cheese
1   egg plus 1 eggwhite

plain flour
oil for frying

The Filling

1½   cups grated feta cheese
     dash of cayenne pepper
2   tablespoons finely chopped green onions
2   oz (55 gr) cream cheese
1/2   cup grated Parmesan or Romano cheese
1   teaspoon oregano or
     pinch of mint or basil

Peel the eggplant and slice lengthwise, ¼ inch (0.5 cm) thick. Sprinkle with a little salt and set aside for one hour. Rinse off salt with plenty of water and drain well, pressing lightly between your palms. Fry the eggplant lightly in olive oil and drain on paper towels, to absorb excess oil. Mix the ingredients for the filling together in a bowl. In a shallow bowl, mix the dry bread crumbs with the Parmesan. In another shallow bowl or a deep plate, beat together the egg, egg white, and 1 tablespoon olive oil. Place one teaspoon of the cheese filling at the end of each strip of eggplant and roll up. If the strips are too long, cut in half and make two rolls from each one. Roll in flour, dip in the beaten egg, and dredge in bread crumbs. Arrange on a platter and cool in the refrigerator before sealing in a plastic bag. Freeze until ready to use. When ready to serve, fry 4-5 minutes in a deep fryer and serve hot.

Preparation time 2 hours

Miniature Stuffed Tomatoes and Peppers

20   small tomatoes
20   small green bell peppers
2   medium onions, grated and rinsed in water
1/2   cup olive oil
1   cup tomato juice
1/2   cup finely chopped parsley
      dash of cayenne pepper
1   teaspoon sugar
1   cup beef stock
      salt and pepper, to taste
1½   cups long-grain rice
2   oz (50 gr) pine nuts
1/4   cup black currants
      white pepper for garnish

Wash the tomatoes and peppers well and wipe. Slice off the bottom ends and scoop out the pepper seeds and the tomato pulp. Press the pulp through a sieve. Saute the onion in the oil, add the tomato juice along with the strained tomato pulp and simmer for 30 minutes. Add the parsley, hot pepper, sugar, beef stock, salt, and freshly ground pepper; continue cooking for another 20 minutes. Remove from the heat and stir in the rice, the pine nuts, and currants. Half-fill the tomatoes and peppers, and place in a greased ovenproof dish with the open end down. Rinse out the saucepan with a little water and pour over the stuffed vegetables. Dribble a little olive oil all over and sprinkle with salt and white pepper. Bake in a 400 °F (200 °C) oven for about 1 hour. Cool and transfer to a platter, with cut side up. Serve cold.

Preparation time 2 hours and 30 minutes

Seafood Parcels

1   lb (450 gr) shrimps
8   oz (250 gr) crabmeat
2   cups water
2   cups finely chopped celery
4-5   very thin green onions, tops only
3   tablespoons whipping cream
1   small clove of garlic
      salt and pepper, to taste
10   sheets phyllo
1/2   cup clarified butter or margarine, melted

The Sauce

1   tablespoon lemon juice
1/3   cup whipping cream
2   egg yolks
2   tablespoons butter
1   tablespoon finely chopped green onions
1   tablespoon finely chopped parsley

Clean and devein the shrimp; rinse and drain well. Place the water and the celery in a saucepan and bring to a boil. Add the shrimp and crabmeat and blanch for 30 seconds. Remove with a slotted spoon and set aside. In the same pan blanch the onion tops 1-2 minutes until slightly wilted. Remove with slotted spoon and set aside. Strain the broth, set 1/3 cup aside for the sauce and discard the rest. Finely chop the shrimp and crab; mix with the cream, garlic, salt and pepper. Cut the phyllo sheets in half lengthwise. Brush the top half with melted butter and fold the other half over it. Brush again with butter, place a tablespoonful of the seafood filling on the bottom end of each phyllo half, and roll up. Slightly twist ends and tie with the blanched onion tops. Arrange on a buttered baking sheet. Brush rolls with melted butter and bake in a 350°F (180°C) oven 10-15 minutes, until lightly browned. Meanwhile, prepare the sauce. Combine the lemon juice, cream and egg yolks with the reserved broth. Stir the sauce over low heat until heated to the boiling point. Stir in the butter a little at a time and continue stirring, until the sauce thickens slightly. Stir in the chopped onions, parsley, salt and pepper. Serve hot with the seafood rolls.

Preparation time 1 hour and 30 minutes

Orange Punch

8   cups reconstituted frozen orange juice
6   cups orange soda
2   lemons, juice and peel
1   cup gin
30 ice cubes

The day before the party, chill the orange juice and soda in the refrigerator. Shortly before the guests are due to arrive, mix all the ingredients except for the ice cubes in a glass punch bowl. With a peel stripper, pull off spiral strips of the lemon peel before squeezing it and place in the punch bowl. Add ice cubes just before serving so as not to dilute the punch. Or put 2-3 ice cubes in each glass when it is served. Garnish each glass with a slice of orange.

Preparation time 5 minutes

Carnival Salad Bar

A salad bar gives you the opportunity to improvise with seasonal vegetables. Most vegetables can be eaten raw. Broccoli, celery, carrots, tomatoes, cucumbers, lettuce, endive, mushrooms, rocket, spinach, asparagus, purslane, cauliflower, cabbage, and radishes make up a wide selection to choose from. Cooked vegetables such as string beans, peas, potatoes can supplement the fresh. Take care not to overcook. And don't forget the onions, green or dry; they lend a particular piquancy to any salad. From the legume family, chickpeas, white and red beans, and even lentils make excellent partners for fresh vegetables. Croutons, fried bacon bits, cubes of soft cheese, or grated hard cheeses as well as dried nuts and fruits can also be included. Necessary to every salad is, of course, the dressing. Be sure to provide at least three different choices of dressing, to satisfy every taste. Choose from the following classic recipes; each one yields one cup of dressing. Serve the dressing in small bowls, each with its own serving spoon.

Italian Dressing

In a small jar vigorously shake $2/3$ cup olive oil, $1/3$ cup white vinegar, 1 pressed clove of garlic, 2 tablespoons of finely chopped onion, 1 tablespoon chopped pimiento, salt and freshly ground black pepper.

French Dressing

In a small jar, vigorously shake $2/3$ cup olive oil, $1/3$ cup white vinegar, $1/2$ teaspoon powdered mustard, salt, and freshly ground pepper, to taste. If desired, you can add 1 teaspoon curry powder and 2 green onions, finely chopped.

Blue Cheese Dressing

Mash 2-3 oz (75 gr) blue cheese with 2-3 tablespoons whipping cream in the blender. Add $1/4$ cup vinegar and $1/4$ cup lemon juice; process until well blended. Remove the cap and processing on high, add $1/2$ cup olive oil in a continuous thin stream; continue processing until the mixture is smooth and creamy.

Herbed Dressing

In a small jar, shake vigorously $3/4$ cup olive oil, $1/4$ cup vinegar, 1 tablespoon finely chopped basil, 1 tablespoon finely chopped parsley, $1/2$ teaspoon oregano, salt, and freshly ground black pepper, to taste.

Hot and Sour Dressing

In a small jar, shake vigorously $1/2$ cup olive oil, $1/4$ cup vinegar, $1/4$ cup chili sauce, 1 teaspoon sugar, salt and freshly ground pepper, to taste.

Pepper Dressing

In a small jar, shake vigorously $1/2$ cup olive oil, $1/4$ cup lemon juice, 1 small mashed clove of garlic, $1/2$ teaspoon oregano, 2 teaspoons green peppercorns, 1 tablespoon Dijon mustard, salt, and freshly ground black pepper, to taste.

Pumpkin Basket with Fresh Fruit

Decoratively cut a large squash or pumpkin in half and fill with fresh fruit following the directions given on page 19. The perfect centerpiece for your carnival buffet.

Bread Basket

Prepare bread dough according to the recipe of your choice. Form dinner rolls in various shapes and sprinkle with several different toppings such as poppy seeds, onion seeds or sesame seeds (pages 42, 95, 182). Attractively arrange in a basket appropriately decorated for the occasion.

Risotto with Squid

1/3   cup olive oil
2   cloves garlic, thinly sliced
1   lb (450 gr) squid, sliced in thin strips
8   oz (250 gr) fresh mushrooms, thinly sliced
1   cup beef stock
2½   cups hot water
   salt and pepper, to taste
1/8   teaspoon cayenne pepper
2   cups long-grain rice
32   cooked shrimp

Heat the oil in a pan and saute the garlic until it begins to brown. Remove garlic and discard. In the same oil, add the squid and mushrooms, and stir while cooking over high heat, until nearly all the liquid has been evaporated and only the oil remains. Add the stock, the water, salt, and pepper; bring to a boil and stir in the rice. Cover, reduce heat, and simmer until all the liquid has been absorbed and the rice is tender, about 20 minutes. Transfer to an ovenproof ring mold and press down so the rice takes the shape of the mold. Cover and refrigerate. Shortly before serving, cover the mold containing the rice with aluminum foil and heat in a 300° (150°C) oven until heated through. Unmold rice on a platter and surround with cooked shrimp and fresh vegetables. Garnish the rice ring with tiny bunches of carrot strips, tied with blanched green onion tops.

Preparation time 1 hour

Carnival Cheese Platter

Place a variety of cheeses on a wooden platter. For a carnival note, create a "clown's head" cheese ball. With a special garland-cutter tool, make serpentines from cucumber and garnish the platter.

Cheese Clown

14   oz (400 gr) cream cheese or ricotta cheese
2   cups grated Cheddar cheese
1   tablespoon finely chopped onion
2   teaspoons Worcestershire sauce
1   teaspoon lemon juice
1/8   teaspoon cayenne pepper
   salt and pepper, to taste

1   tablespoon finely chopped red pepper
1   tablespoon finely chopped green pepper
1   large fresh red bell pepper
2-3   cucumbers

Put the cheese in the mixing bowl of an electric mixer and allow to soften at room temperature. Add the onion, Worcestershire sauce, lemon juice, cayenne, salt, and freshly ground pepper. Beat at low speed until light and smooth. Blend in the chopped peppers. Cover and refrigerate until firm. Shape into a ball and refrigerate again. From fresh red pepper, cut ears, mouth, nose, and pointed cap; place on the cheese ball, transforming it into a clown. For eyes, use halves of a black olive and a spiral-cut cucumber garland for the clown's collar.

Preparation time 15 minutes

Organizing your Carnival Buffet Party

Organize a friendly carnival buffet in your home for 16 persons. Greet your guests with an apéritif of orange punch accompanied by smoked salmon rolls or rosettes on ice with small rolls of fresh butter, finely chopped onion which they can serve themselves on Melba toast. In keeping with the carnival spirit, decorate your buffet with a funny penguin cut from a large eggplant and the cheese ball clown. This buffet menu calls for a light rosé or dry white wine.

❀ *Each recipe serves 16 persons.*
❀ *Well in advance, prepare the eggplant croquettes, the seafood wrapped in phyllo, the bread rolls, and the ice cream tartlets. Store in the freezer.*
❀ *Two days in advance, prepare the cannoli, without the filling.*
❀ *The morning before, prepare the cheese ball, the stuffed tomatoes and peppers, and the pumpkin basket with fresh fruit. Fold the napkins into holders for the knives and forks and roll paper napkins into cones, placing them in a small vase or bowl.*
❀ *The evening before, clean and cut the squid. Cook and clean the shrimp and refrigerate. Prepare the fixings for the salad bar except for the mushrooms, and set the buffet.*
❀ *During the day, prepare the risotto, the cheeses and garnishes for the cheese board, and the fresh mushrooms for the salad bar. Fill the cannoli.*
❀ *Shortly before the guests arrive, prepare the punch.*

Ice Cream Tartlets

30   chocolate tartlets
4   egg yolks
1/2   cup sugar
2   cups whipping cream
2   tablespoons instant coffee
2   tablespoons hot milk
2   tablespoons whiskey

      The Garnish
1   cup whipping cream
1/2   teaspoon vanilla extract
1   egg white
2   tablespoons sugar
1-2   oz (50 gr) semi-sweet baking chocolate, melted
      red and green maraschino cherries

Prepare the tartlets from semi-sweet white and dark chocolate as in the recipe "Chocolate Tarts with Mint Mousse" (page 94). You can fill the tartlets with store bought ice cream, vanilla for the dark tartlets and chocolate for the white ones (one pint each). If you have time, you can prepare this easy mocha ice cream filling. Beat the egg yolks and the sugar with the mixer, at high speed, until light and fluffy. Meanwhile scald the cream and with the mixer on, add it slowly in a thin steady stream into the egg mixture. Continue beating, until thick. Pour into a metal ice cream box and chill slightly in the freezer. Return to the mixing bowl and beat again until light and increased in bulk. Fill the tartlets and freeze. Meanwhile, prepare the garnish; whip the cream with the vanilla until stiff. In a separate bowl beat the egg white with the sugar to a stiff meringue and fold into the whipped cream. Divide in half; set aside one portion in the refrigerator. To the other half, add the cooled melted chocolate and chill. Using two separate pastry bags fitted with star tips, garnish the dark tartlets with white rosettes and the white ones with dark rosettes. Garnish half and half with pieces of red and green maraschino cherries. Cover tightly with plastic wrap, and freeze, until ready to serve. They will keep for 6 months.

Preparation time 4 hours

Cannoli ala Siciliana

The Pastry
2   cups all purpose flour
2   eggs plus 2 yolks
1   teaspoon lemon zest
2   teaspoons sherry or port wine
1   egg white, lightly beaten
     corn oil for frying

The Filling
1   lb (500 gr) ricotta cheese
1   cup powdered sugar
1½   teaspoons cinnamon
1   teaspoon lemon zest
1/3 cup finely chopped mixed candied peel
     powdered sugar for dusting
     grated chocolate or sprinkles

The Pastry: Mix the dough ingredients except for the beaten egg white, and knead well until smooth and stiff. Cover with plastic wrap and refrigerate the dough for 1 hour. Divide into 2 or 3 parts, and roll out each one as thin as a sheet of paper. The thinner the pastry is, the lighter and crisper the cannoli will be when fried in oil. If you have a pasta-maker, pass the dough through it 3 times. Cut the pastry into 2½ inch (6-7 cm) wide strips. Cut these into pieces long enough to be wound around the metal cannoli tubes with a ½ inch (1 cm) overlap. Brush the overlapping edges with the beaten egg white so they stick together. Deep fry in hot oil for about 1 minute, until lightly browned. Cool slightly on paper towels and with a paper napkin, carefully pull off the tubes and allow the cannoli to cool completely.

The Filling: In a mixing bowl combine the cheese and sugar; beat at high speed for 5 minutes until light and creamy. Add the cinnamon and zest; continue beating another 2 minutes. Fold in the candied fruit peel. Fill the cannoli with the cream mixture using a pastry bag fitted with a plain wide tip. Dip the ends in a plate of grated chocolate or sprinkles. Roll in powdered sugar. Alternatively, mix half the filling with 3-4 oz (100 gr) melted semi-sweet baking chocolate and fill half the cannolli. Refrigerate uncovered. Yield 40 pieces.

Preparation time 2 hours

REUNION DINNER

MENU

Hot Canapés or
Prosciutto with Melon and Figs

❧

Avocado with Crab or Onion Soup

❧

Veal Roll Stuffed with Spinach
Fried Potato Baskets, Potato Croquettes

❧

Hot Tomato Salad

❧

Cheese Platter

❧

Ice Cream in Brandy Snap Baskets,
Banana Fritters or Cappuccino Soufflé

❧

White and Dry Red Wine

Hot Canapés

With Salmon & Mozzarella

16   round canapés
4   tablespoons soft butter
      a bit of mashed garlic
1/2   teaspoon prepared mustard
1   tablespoon finely chopped parsley
2   teaspoons capers, mashed
4   large slices of mozzarella cheese, quartered
4   large sliced smoked salmon, quartered

Combine the butter with garlic, mustard, parsley, and capers. Spread a little of the mixture on one side of the canapés. Put a piece of salmon on each and top with a piece of cheese. Arrange the canapés in a baking pan and bake in a 375°F (180°C) oven for 10 minutes, or until the cheese melts. Serve immediately.

With Smoked Trout

18   triangular canapés
7   oz (200 gr) smoked trout
3   tablespoons soft butter
2   green onions, finely chopped

1   teaspoon flour
1/4   cup whipping cream
1/2   teaspoon prepared mustard
      salt and pepper
2   tablespoons Parmesan cheese

Mash the trout with a fork. Melt the butter in a pan, add the onion and saute for 1 minute. Stir in the flour and saute for another minute. Stir in the cream, salt, pepper, and the mustard; cook until sauce thickens slightly. Remove from the heat and mix in the mashed trout. Spread the canapés with the trout filling and sprinkle with a little Parmesan. Garnish with thin strips of green pepper and arrange in a baking pan. Bake in a 350°F (180°C) oven for 10 minutes and serve hot.

Preparation time 45 minutes

Prosciutto with Melon and Figs

1   medium cantelope or honey dew melon
11   oz (300 gr) prosciutto
6   figs

With a melon baller, cut small balls from the melon. Cut the prosciutto in strips and roll into rosettes. Wash and wipe

40

the figs. Cut in quarters lengthwise from the top, without separating the pieces at the bottom. Arrange the fruit and the prosciutto on a round platter and cover with plastic wrap. Refrigerate until ready to serve.

Preparation time 30 minutes

Avocado with Crab

4	large ripe avocados
1/4	cup lemon juice
	salt and white pepper
1	lb (½ kg) frozen crabmeat, chopped
4	green onions, finely chopped
1	celery stalk, finely chopped
1/2	cup Parmesan or mild kefalotiri cheese

The Dressing

1/4	cup butter
1/4	cup flour
2/3	cup milk
2/3	cup whipping cream
2	tablespoons ketchup
1/4	teaspoon curry powder
2	tablespoons mayonnaise

Cut the avocados in half lengthwise and twist to separate. Carefully remove the pits with the tip of a knife. Brush the surface of the avocados with lemon juice, to prevent discoloration. Slice a bit off the bottoms (uncut sides) so they will sit on the plate without tipping. Sprinkle with salt and white pepper. In a bowl, mix the crab with the onion, celery, salt, and pepper. Divide evenly and heap on the 8 avocado halves. Arrange in a baking dish with 1 inch (2 cm) of cold water. Set aside. Saute the flour in the butter, add

the milk and cream and prepare the bechamel sauce. When it is thick, remove from the heat, cool slightly, and stir in ketchup, curry powder, and mayonnaise. If desired, stir in half the Parmesan. Put 2-3 tablespoons of sauce on each avocado, on top of the filling, and sprinkle with the remaining Parmesan. Bake in a 400°F (200°C) over for 15 minutes. Serve immediately. Do not overcook or reheat the avocados or they will taste bitter.

Preparation time 1 hour

Onion Soup

4	large onions, thinly sliced
4	tablespoons butter
2	tablespoons flour
8	cups hot meat stock (or water)
8	slices of stale white bread
7	oz (200 gr) grated Emmentaler cheese
	salt and pepper

Melt the butter in a saucepan and add the onions. Sprinkle with a little salt, cover and simmer over low heat, stirring occasionally, for about 40 minutes, until transparent. Uncover, add the flour and increase the heat. Saute the onions, stirring continuously, until they are golden brown, about 30 minutes. If they start to brown too quickly, lower the heat. Add the stock or water and simmer for 10 minutes. Add salt and freshly ground black pepper and divide the soup among 8 ovenproof bowls. Put a slice of bread in each and sprinkle with the grated cheese. Put the bowls under the broiler, until the cheese melts and browns slightly. Serve the soup immediately.

Preparation time 1 hour 40 minutes

Bread Pretzels

2	lbs (1kg) all-purpose flour
2	tablespoons dry active yeast or
2	oz (60 gr) compressed yeast
1 ½	cups warm water 100°F (40°C)
1/4	cup sugar
1/4	cup corn oil
2	teaspoons salt
3	eggs, slightly beaten
1	egg white, lightly beaten with
1	tablespoon water
	coarse salt or sesame seeds

In a mixing bowl, combine ⅔ of the flour with the yeast. Add the sugar, corn oil, salt, eggs, and the warm water. Beat at medium speed for a few seconds. Then beat at high speed for 3 minutes. Add as much flour as needed to make a stiff dough. Knead the dough for 6-8 minutes, until smooth and elastic. Allow to rise in a warm place, until doubled in bulk, about 1 hour and 30 minutes. Punch down the dough, cover, and let stand for ten minutes. On a lightly floured worktop, roll the dough into a rectangle, 10x12 inches (25x30 cm). Cut strips ⅔ inch (1.5 cm) wide and roll each one into 16-inch (40 cm) length. Twist the strips into pretzels and arrange on a greased baking sheet. Cover and allow to rise. Brush with the beaten egg white. Sprinkle them lightly with coarse salt or sesame seeds, and bake in a 350°F (175°C) oven for 20-25 minutes, or until golden brown. Cool on a wire rack. Rolls may be frozen until ready to serve.

Preparation time 3 hours

Veal Roll Stuffed with Spinach

3	lb (1½ kg) breast of veal, deboned and flattened
1	lb (1/2 kg) spinach, washed and chopped
1/4	cup butter
2	tablespoons grated onion
	salt and pepper
3	eggs
2	tablespoons milk
3	tablespoons grated Parmesan cheese
1/4	cup butter
1/2	cup white wine

Blanch the spinach, drain, and gently squeeze out excess liquid, pressing between your palms. Heat the butter in a saucepan and lightly saute the onion and the spinach, stirring over high heat for 5 minutes. Add salt and freshly ground black pepper, and spread over the meat. In a bowl, beat the eggs and stir in the milk and cheese. Melt 3 tablespoons of butter in a large frying pan and pour the egg mixture into it. Fry and turn the omelette over onto the spinach filling. Sprinkle with a little salt and freshly ground pepper. Roll up tightly from the long edge and tie securely with string. Melt ¼ cup butter in a large pan and saute the rolled veal until lightly browned on all sides. Pour the wine, over it cover, and simmer for about 2 hours, adding a little water at intervals, until the meat is tender and the sauce

has thickened. Lift out the veal, remove the string and slice. If there is not enough sauce, add one cup of meat stock with 1 teaspoon cornstarch and cook until thick. Arrange the sliced veal on a platter with fried carrots and potatoes in fried string potato baskets. Serve the sauce separately in a gravy boat.

Preparation time 3 hours

Potato Croquettes

3	large potatoes, cooked
2	oz (50 gr) cream cheese
1/4	cup grated Parmesan cheese
1/4	cup whipping cream
2	tablespoons grated onion
1	egg yolk
	salt and pepper
1	egg white lightly beaten with 2 tablespoons oil
1	cup finely crushed corn flakes

Mash the cooked potatoes with the cheeses, cream, onion, egg yolk, salt, and pepper. If the mixture is too soft, add more Parmesan. If it is too stiff, add a little cream. Refrigerate until firm enough to shape into little balls. Roll the balls first in the egg white, and then in the corn flakes. Arrange the croquettes on a platter and chill. Seal in airtight plastic bags and freeze. When ready to serve, arrange on a greased baking sheet and bake in a 400°F (200°C) oven for about 30 minutes. Alternatively, fry in hot oil.

Preparation time 2 hours

Organizing your Reunion Dinner

Invite an beloved old friend for a warm reunion dinner party. Include a few mutual friends for an evening of reminiscing over good food and wine. The menu suggested here is perfect for such an occasion. Instead of the avocado with crab, you may serve the onion soup or vegetable consommé. Serve dry white wine with the avocado and a full-bodied red wine with the rolled veal.

❋ *Each recipe serves eight persons.*
❋ *Well in advance, make the pretzels, and the potato croquettes and freeze them.*
❋ *The morning before, make the brandy-snap baskets, the caramel sauce and the fried potato baskets. Seal them tightly in plastic bags and store in a cool dry place.*
❋*The afternoon before, prepare the canapés and salad without baking. Cut and blanch the carrot and potato balls. Store in the refrigerator.*
❋ *The evening before, prepare the rolled veal and saute. Cool and refrigerate. It should be cooked the day of the party.*
❋ *In the morning, prepare the prosciutto platter. Stuff the avocados, but don't bake them. Refrigerate until ready to serve. They should be cooked shortly before serving. Prepare the cappuccino soufflé to the stage specified in the recipe. You can also prepare the sauces.*
❋ *Shortly before, serving fry the croquettes and the carrots, bake the avocados.*
❋ *Before serving the desserts, finish the soufflé, bake and serve immediately.*

Fried Potato Baskets

To make the baskets, you will need a double wire mesh basket. You can use two separate wire mesh strainers, one slightly smaller than the other. Peel 4-5 medium potatoes and coarsely shred in the food processor, pushing down the potato with the plunger to make long potato "strings". Pat dry between paper towels and toss with a little cornstarch. Evenly arrange the raw potato strings in the large strainer and press the small strainer on top. Deep fry in hot oil until the potatoes are golden brown. Separate the two strainers and carefully remove the basket. Let it drain on paper towels. Repeat until all the baskets have been prepared. The baskets can be fried one day in advance. Fill them with fried carrot and potato balls shortly before serving. The carrot and potato balls will fry more quickly if they are first blanched in boiling water for a few minutes. Drain, roll in flour and fry. Alternatively, you can serve the potato croquettes in the baskets.

Preparation time 2 hours

Hot Tomato Salad

1	small cucumber, thinly sliced
3	tomatoes, thinly sliced
3	tablespoons olive oil
2	tablespoons lemon juice
1	small clove of garlic, mashed
2	tablespoons finely chopped parsley
4	tablespoons grated kefalotiri or Parmesan cheese
1	tablespoon finely chopped mint

Place one cucumber slice on each tomato slice. Place the cucumber-tomato slices overlapping each other in a round ovenproof dish. Beat the olive oil with the lemon juice, mashed garlic, and the parsley for one minute. Pour over the salad and sprinkle with the grated cheese. Cover and refrigerate. Shortly before serving, place under broiler until cheese melts. Sprinkle with the mint and serve immediately.

Preparation time 30 minutes

Cheese Platter

Choose 5 or 6 kinds of cheese such as Gouda, boursin, Emmentaler, Brie, smoked Metsovo cheese, blue cheese, or feta cheese. Arrange attractively on a cheese platter or board so the guests can easily serve themselves. Garnish with fresh figs, green and red grapes, or other fresh seasonal fruits.

Custard Sauce

Heat 1 cup of milk in a double boiler until it starts to bubble. Beat the 2 egg yolks (left over from the Cappuccino Soufflé recipe) with 2 tablespoons of sugar and $1/8$ teaspoon salt. Stirring vigorously, slowly add the hot milk. Return mixture to the double boiler, and continue stirring over the hot water (simmering), until custard is thick enough to coat the spoon. Add $1/2$ teaspoon vanilla extract and empty into a bowl. Cover the surface with a piece of plastic wrap to prevent a crust from forming and allow to cool. Refrigerate until ready to serve.

Coffee Cream

Dissolve 2 teaspoons instant coffee in one teaspoon cold water and add 1 teaspoon Kahlua. Put in a mixing bowl along with $1/2$ cup whipping cream and 2 tablespoons powdered sugar. Beat at medium speed, until the mixture is slightly thick and fluffy. Cover and refrigerate. Sprinkle with a little instant coffee, if desired, just before serving.

Cappuccino Soufflé

7	oz (200 gr) semi-sweet baking chocolate
3/4	cup whipping cream
3	egg yolks, lightly beaten
1/3	cup evaporated milk
4	teaspoons cornstarch
1	tablespoon instant coffee
1	teaspoon vanilla extract
5	egg whites
1	teaspoon cream of tartar
1/4	cup sugar

Melt the chocolate in a double boiler or over very low heat. Lightly beat the whipping cream with the egg yolks and fold into the melted chocolate. Dissolve the cornstarch, the vanilla, and the instant coffee in the milk and stir into the chocolate mixture. This may be done in advance and kept covered in the refrigerator until ready to use. Remove from the refrigerator several hours before making the souffle and allow the mixture to come to room temperature. Beat the egg whites with the cream of tartar until foamy. Beating continuously, add the sugar a little at a time, until the mixture holds soft peaks. Carefully fold the meringue into the chocolate mixture. Pour into a 7-cup soufflé dish. Bake in a 350 °F (180 °C) oven for 40-45 minutes. Sprinkle the surface with powdered sugar and serve immediately, accompanied by the custard sauce or the coffee cream.

Preparation time 1 hour

Ice Cream in Brandy Snap Baskets

1   recipe for "Brandy Snaps" (page 130)
1   qt (1 kg) vanilla ice cream
2   cups (250 gr) whipped cream
     banana fritters

Prepare the brandy snaps according to the recipe. While the wafers are still warm, place in custard cups, shaping them into "baskets". When completely cool, cover with plastic wrap and store in a cool dry place for up to one day in advance. Just before serving, place a scoop of ice cream in each basket and garnish with a whipped cream rosette. Accompany with caramelized banana fritters.

Preparation time 1 hour

Caramel Sauce

1   cup sugar
1/4 cup water
1   cup whipping cream
1/2 teaspoon vanilla extract

In a heavy-bottomed saucepan, melt the sugar in the water over high heat. Do not stir the mixture, just swirl the pan. Boil until the sugar becomes the color of maple syrup. Be careful not to burn the sugar. Remove from the heat and whisk in the whipping cream and the vanilla. Allow the sauce to cool and refrigerate in a jar until ready to use.

Preparation time 15 minutes

Banana Fritters

4   large bananas
     lemon juice
     The Batter
1/2 cup all purpose flour
     pinch of salt
1   tablespoon salad oil
1/2 cup soda water
1   egg white
     The Caramel Syrup
1½   cups sugar
1/4 cup water
1/8 teaspoon cream of tartar

Mix all the batter ingredients except for the egg white. Beat for 1 minute until smooth and set aside for 1 hour. Beat the egg whites into a soft meringue and fold into the batter. Boil the syrup ingredients in a small saucepan, until a golden brown caramel is formed. Remove from the heat and whisk in $1/3$ cup water. Return to heat and stir, until the caramel melts and forms a medium thick syrup. Set aside to cool. Meanwhile, peel and cut the bananas into 5 or 6 pieces, $1\frac{1}{2}$ inch each. Sprinkle with lemon juice to prevent discoloration. Dip the banana pieces into the batter and fry in hot oil. Remove with a slotted spoon and dip briefly into the syrup. Serve with ice cream.

Preparation time 1 hour and 30 minutes

EASTER WITH THE FAMILY

MENU

Stuffed Easter Eggs
Easter Potato Salad

❧

Lamb Sundry Surprise

❧

Stuffed Breast of Spring Lamb

❧

Salad Nicoise

❧

Easter Bread Ring

❧

Raspberry Cheesecake or
Meringues with Strawberries

❧

Strawberry Bonbons or
Pear Tart

❧

Petite Sirah or
Grande Reserve Greek Wine

Stuffed Easter Eggs

8   hard boiled eggs
1/4 cup mayonnaise
1   teaspoon prepared mustard
1   teaspoon capers
1   teaspoon finely chopped green pepper
     salt and freshly ground black pepper
1   tablespoon finely chopped green onion
8   cocktail onions
1   small carrot stick

Stuffed-egg Mimosas: Peel the eggs; slice a bit off the tops and bottoms so they can be placed on end when cut in half crosswise. Carefully remove the yolks. Put 6 yolks in the food processor with the remaining ingredients and beat lightly until blended. Stuff the egg cups, heaping the filling above the rims. Finely grate a little of the remaining yolks on top, to resemble mimosa blossoms.

Stuffed-egg Ducklings: Divide the eggs in half lengthwise. Prepare the filling as above, using all the egg yolks. With a pastry bag fitted with a star tip, stuff the whites with the yolk mixture. Slice narrow pieces lengthwise from one or two whites and place two on each stuffed egg so they resemble wings. With the tip of a sharp knife, make a small cut on the surface of the cocktail onion, push in a tiny carrot "beak" and using toothpicks, attach the duckling's "head" to each

egg. The stuffed-egg ducklings, attractively arranged on a small plate, will particularly delight the children at your Easter table. You can decorate other Easter eggs with simple materials on hand as in the photograph.

Easter Potato Salad

8   *strips of bacon, chopped*
5   *cups of chopped boiled potatoes*
1/2 *cup finely chopped celery*
1/4 *cup grated kefalotiri or Parmesan cheese*
2   *green onions, finely chopped*
1/4 *cup finely cut dill pickles*
2   *tablespoons finely chopped red bell pepper*
2   *tablespoons finely chopped green pepper*
2   *tablespoons finely chopped parsley*
     salt and pepper, to taste
4   *tablespoons olive oil*
2   *tablespoons vinegar*
2   *tablespoons mayonnaise*
1   *teaspoon horseradish*
4   *tablespoons lemon juice*
2   *teaspoons prepared mustard*
7   *oz (200 gr) softened cream cheese*
2   *red bell peppers for garnish*

Saute the bacon on medium heat until brown and crisp. Drain on paper towels. In a large bowl, combine the potatoes with the bacon and the next 8 ingredients. Put the oil, vinegar, the mayonnaise, horseradish, lemon juice, mustard, and the cream cheese in a food processor. Beat for 1 minute until smooth. Pour over potatoes and toss. Empty into a 6-cup ring mold lined with plastic wrap. Refrigerate overnight. Unmold on a round platter, carefully remove plastic wrap, and garnish with red pepper strips. Surround with curly endive and the mimosa eggs.

Preparation time 1 hour

Multi-Colored Easter Eggs

Put one layer of eggs in the bottom of a large pot and cover with cold water. Bring to a boil, lower heat and simmer for 10 minutes. Carefully remove with a slotted spoon and put in cold water to cool, so they will peel easily. Set aside, and refrigerate those which have cracked to use for the stuffed-egg recipes. Divide the uncracked eggs into 4-5 parts, or as many colors as you wish to dye the eggs. Following the directions on the package of dye, color your eggs red, blue, yellow, green or orange. Food coloring in liquid or paste form may also be used. Follow the directions given on the box.

Preparation time 2 hours

Lamb Sundry Surprise

1   spring lamb offal (heart, livers, sweet breads
      about 3 lbs (1½ kg)
1   lb (500 gr) lamb intestines (or lamb livers)
4   lbs (2 kg) green onions
1/2 cup olive oil
2   tablespoons finely chopped fresh dill
1   tablespoon finely chopped fresh mint
      salt and pepper, to taste
1/3 cup butter or margarine
6-7 phyllo sheets

Blanch the lamb offal, drain and chop into bite-sized pieces. Clean and wash the intestines well; blanch, drain and chop finely. If not available, you may omit the intestines and increase the quantity of the offal accordingly. Clean the green onions, cut into 1½ inch pieces and blanch. In a large heavy pan combine the chopped offal with the intestines and the onions. Pour in the oil, cover and simmer until tender. Add a little water, if necessary. When almost all the juice has evaporated, add the dill, mint, salt, and freshly ground pepper. Turn into a 10-inch (25-cm) ovenproof dish. Lay one sheet of phyllo on the surface of the dish and trim to size; brush with melted butter and slash the center open. Open another sheet of phyllo on the work surface and brush the half lengthwise with butter. Fold the other half over the buttered part; cut along the fold to separate. Brush with butter. Ruffle and place on top of baking dish along outer edge. Repeat making more phyllo ruffles, to cover the entire surface. Brush the phyllo ruffles liberally with butter. Bake in a 400 °F (200 °C) oven for 30-35 minutes, until the phyllo is golden brown. Serve hot.

Preparation time 2 hours and 30 minutes

Salad Nicoise

1/2 lb (250 gr) fresh string beans
1/2 lb (250 gr) potatoes, cubed
6   medium tomatoes, sliced
10   green stuffed olives
10   black olives
8   anchovy fillets

The Dressing
4   tablespoons olive oil
2   tablespoons vinegar
1/2 teaspoon tarragon
1   tablespoon finely chopped parsley
1   tablespoon fine capers
      salt and black pepper

Wash and trim the green beans, cut into pieces and cook in salted water until soft; drain and set aside. Cook the potatoes in salted water; drain and set aside to cool. Attractively arrange the ingredients for the salad on a platter, cover with plastic wrap and refrigerate. Shortly before serving, shake the dressing ingredients in a small jar and pour over the salad. Serve immediately.

Preparation time 20 minutes

Organizing your Easter with the Family

Easter is the most important Spring holiday, the greatest feast of Christianity. Roll up your sleeves and prepare these suggested variations of traditional Greek Easter recipes. Gather your family around a gaily decorated Easter table, filled with flowers and the colors of Spring. Dye eggs many colors and prepare stuffed-egg ducklings for the youngsters. Prepare an Easter bread ring filled with chocolate and almonds. Its rich flavor and spectacular appearance will delight young and old alike. Dry red wine is an excellent choice to accompany this special Greek Easter dinner.

❧ Each recipe serves 8 persons.
❧ Well in advance, prepare the rolls, the Easter ring, the meringues, dill and securely tie the breast of lamb. Store according to the recommendations in the recipes.
❧ Three days in advance, dye the eggs and make the strawberry bonbons.
❧ The morning before, make the raspberry cheesecake or the pear tart, fix the potato salad and store everything in the refrigerator. Sandwich the pairs of meringues together with the whipped cream and strawberries and refrigerate uncovered.
❧ The afternoon before, cook the lamb sundries with the onions, place in an ovenproof dish, cover with the phyllo ruffles and refrigerate. Take the lamb out of the freezer.
❧ During the day, remove the rolls and the Easter ring from the freezer. Cut the potatoes and roast with the lamb in the oven.
❧ Shortly before serving, bake the lamb sundry surprise. Happy Easter.

Strawberry Bonbons

5   oz (150 gr) grated coconut
5   oz (150 gr) almonds, blanched and ground
4   tablespoons sugar
1   envelope of strawberry gelatin
1   can condensed milk
1   teaspoon vanilla extract

in a bowl, combine the coconut, almonds, sugar, vanilla and
$3/4$ of the gelatin. Add enough condensed milk to bind the
ingredients in a stiff pliable mixture. In a small bowl combine
the rest of the gelatin with 4 tablespoons pink sugar. With
the first mixture shape strawberries and roll them in the
sugar mixture. Make small leaves from angelica and place
two on each strawberry. Put the strawberries in fluted candy
cups.

Preparation time 45 minutes

Stuffed Breast of Spring Lamb

1   large breast of spring lamb, 6 lbs (3 kg)
2   tablespoons olive oil
2   tablespoons lemon juice
2   cloves of garlic, mashed
     salt and pepper, to taste

The Stuffing

1/4 cup olive oil
1   cup finely chopped green onions
1   small lamb offal, blanched and finely chopped
     salt and pepper, to taste
1   teaspoon ground green peppercorns
1/3 cup long-grain rice
1   cup beef stock
1/4 cup finely chopped parsley
1/4 cup finely chopped dill
1   teaspoon finely chopped fresh mint
10   medium potatoes
1/2 cup olive oil
1/2 cup Parmesan or kefalotiri cheese

Ask your butcher to prepare a whole lamb breast, cleaning
and cutting the ribs the same length. In a bowl, combine
the oil, lemon juice, garlic, salt, and freshly ground pepper;
liberally brush the meat with this mixture both inside and
out. Put in a large ovenproof roasting pan. Heat the oil in a
saucepan and lightly saute the onion; add and saute the
chopped offal, stirring while cooking, until slightly browned.
Add the salt, black and green pepper, rice, beef stock, and
herbs; mix well and take off the heat. Stuff the breast and
interlace the ribs alternately one between the other. Truss
the breast with string so the sides won't open during
roasting. Cover the ribs with aluminum foil to prevent
burning. Peel the potatoes and slice a piece off the bottoms
as a base to stand them on. With a sharp knife make
slashes $1/8$ inch (0.3 cm) apart cutting through almost to the
base but without separating them. Brush with lemon juice
and set aside for two hours. Brush with oil and arrange
around the lamb in the roasting pan. Place in a slow 300 °F
(150 °C) oven for 1 hour, occasionally basting both the lamb
and the potatoes. Sprinkle the potatoes with grated cheese,
salt, and white pepper. Increase the temperature to 400 °F
(200 °C) and continue roasting until the lamb is done and
the potatoes are golden brown, about 1 hour and 30
minutes. Do not allow pan to dry out; add water, if
necessary.

Preparation time 3-4 hours

Fan Rolls Stuffed with Onions

The Dough

1   recipe for bread (page 163)

The Filling

4   tablespoons olive oil
2   large onions, thinly sliced
     salt and pepper, to taste
1/2 teaspoon ground coriander, thyme or oregano
2   tablespoons dark soya sauce
1   egg yolk beaten with 2 teaspoons water

Prepare the dough as in the recipe, omitting the walnuts.
Allow to rise until doubled in bulk; divide into balls about 1
oz (30 gr) each. To make the filling, heat the oil, and saute
the onion until transparent. Add the salt, pepper and the
herb of your choice. With a rolling pin, flatten the dough
balls slightly into small thick rounds. Brush half the rounds
with the soya sauce and put a little sauteed onion in the
centers. Cover with the remaining rounds and press the
edges together. To be sure the ends stick together, wet with
a little water. With a scissors, make 4 cuts on one side so
the rolls resemble fans. Arrange on a baking sheet lined
with non-stick baking paper. Cover with oiled plastic wrap
and allow to rise about 20 minutes. Brush with the beaten
egg yolk; or, if you prefer, with a little soya sauce which will
give them a dark brown color when baked. Bake in a 400 °F
(200 °C) oven for 20-25 minutes; cool on a rack. Freeze in an
airtight plastic bag until you need them.

Preparation time 3 hours

Easter Bread Ring

The Dough
1½	tablespoons dry yeast
2/3	cup warm milk, 100°F (40°C)
4	cups bread flour
1/3	cup sugar
1	egg plus 2 yolks, lightly beaten
2	tablespoons melted butter
1	teaspoon salt
1/2	cup soft butter, in pats

The Filling
4-5	oz (125 gr) semi-sweet baking chocolate or chips
1/3	cup coarsely chopped blanched almonds
1	egg lightly beaten
1	egg yolk beaten with 1 teaspoon water

Dissolve the yeast in the milk and set aside until foamy, about 10 minutes. Put the flour in a large bowl or basin and make a well in the center. Put in the foamy yeast mixture and the other ingredients, except for the soft butter. Gradually pull in the flour from around the sides of the well, adding extra flour, if necessary, and knead to make a pliable, non-sticky dough. While lightly kneading the dough, add the butter 2 or 3 pats at a time. Always fold the bottom part of the dough over the top, enclosing the butter; continue until all the butter has been incorporated into the dough. Take care not to overwork the dough. Cover and allow to rise in a warm place until doubled in bulk, about 2 hours. Punch down the dough and roll out into a rectangle 8x24 inches (20x60 cm). Brush the surface with the beaten egg; sprinkle the length of half the dough with the chocolate chips and almonds. From the long edge of the same side, roll the dough up and seal the edges brushing with a little water; slightly flatten the roll. Form the roll into a ring and put into a round baking pan lined with non-stick baking paper. Join the ends securely by wetting them and pressing together. Cover and allow the ring to rise in a warm place

for 10 minutes. With a scissors make alternating v-shaped slashes, right and left over the entire surface. Cover and allow to rise another 20 minutes, until doubled in bulk. Brush with egg yolk and bake in a 400°F (200°C) oven for about 20 minutes. Remove from the oven and brush with gelatin glaze as in the recipe, "French Rolls" (page 139).

Preparation time 2 hours and 30 minutes

Pear Tart

The Pastry Crust
1	recipe tart pastry dough
1/2	cup coarsely chopped walnuts

The Filling
11	oz (300 gr) cream cheese
2	eggs
1	cup thick caramel syrup
10	canned pear halves (15 oz can)
1½	cups whipped cream
3	tablespoons coarsely chopped walnuts

Prepare the tart pastry crust as in the recipe "Chocolate Tart" (page 88). Line the bottom and sides of a 10-inch (25-cm) ovenproof tart dish with the pastry. Flute the edges of the pastry with your fingers. Sprinkle the walnuts on the bottom and press into the pastry. Bake in a 400°F (200°C) oven for 10-15 minutes until light brown. Cool and set aside. Meanwhile, prepare the caramel syrup as in the recipe, "Fried bananas"(page 45) and cool. Beat the cream cheese with the eggs and half the syrup; reserve the other half. Pour cheese filling into the baked tart shell. Drain the pears well and arrange on top of the filling. Bake the tart in a 400°F (200°C) oven for 30 minutes. Cool and refrigerate. Shortly before serving, pour the reserved caramel syrup over the tart and garnish with whipped cream rosettes and walnuts.

Preparation time 1 hour and 30 minutes

Meringues with Strawberries

6   egg whites
1/2   teaspoon cream of tartar
1½   cups finely granulated sugar
1   teaspoon vanilla extract
1   lb (250 gr) fresh strawberries or raspberries
1   lb (500 gr) whipped cream
      strawberry or raspberry sauce (page 138)

With the first four ingredients, make the meringue as in the recipe, "Ice Cream Swans" (page 121). Put the meringue in a pastry bag fitted with a large star tip. Lay a sheet of non-stick baking paper on the oven rack and pipe on it, large meringue rosettes 2 inches apart. Allow the meringues to dry out in a 180 °F (80 °C) oven for 1 hour and 30 minutes; turn off, and allow them to cool in the oven. Wash, drain and wipe the strawberries. Cut in small pieces. Join pairs of meringues with whipped cream and strawberries in between. The meringues may be prepared in the morning and stored, uncovered, in the refrigerator. Just before serving, pour the strawberry sauce over them.

Preparation time 2 hours

Raspberry Cheesecake

The Sauce
2   cups fresh or frozen raspberries
3/4   cup sugar
2   tablespoons cornstarch
2   tablespoons lemon juice
2   tablespoons brandy

The Crust
1¼   cups Graham cracker or vanilla cookie crumbs
2   tablespoons sugar
1/4   cup grated almonds or walnuts
1/4   cup melted butter
The Filling
14   oz (400 gr) cream cheese
7   oz (200 gr) ricotta cheese
4   large eggs
2   tablespoons lemon juice
1   teaspoon vanilla extract
1/3   cup all purpose flour
1   tablespoon cornstarch
1/2   cup sugar
4   tablespoons butter
1   cup whipping cream

The Sauce: In a saucepan combine the raspberries, sugar, cornstarch, and lemon juice. Simmer, stirring occasionally, until thick and transparent. Remove from the heat and stir in the brandy. You may substitute strawberries or cherries for the raspberries. The sauce may be prepared when the fruits are in season and frozen until needed, or frozen fruit may be used.

The Crust: Combine the crust ingredients; pat firmly into the bottom and sides of a 12-inch (30-cm) round ovenproof tart or flan dish; Chill in the refrigerator while preparing the filling.

The Filling: In a mixing bowl combine the first 8 filling ingredients. Beat 5 minutes at medium speed. Add the butter and the whipping cream and continue beating for another 5 minutes. Turn into the chilled crust and bake in a 325 °F (160 °C) oven for 1 hour. Turn off the heat and leave the cheesecake to cool in the oven for 2 hours, leaving the door ajar. Spread the raspberry sauce on the surface and garnish the edges with whipped cream rosettes. Refrigerate until ready to serve.

Preparation time 4 hours

MOTHER'S DAY MENU

MENU

Feta Cheese in Phyllo or
Cold Spinach Mousse

❧

Pasta alle Vongole

❧

Salmon Steaks in Wine or
Fillet of Sole with Avocado Sauce
Creamed New Potatoes

❧

Mixed Salad in Glass

❧

Banana Mousse, Rice Pudding or
Tiramisu

❧

Dry White Wine and Champagne

Cold Spinach Mousse

11   oz (300 gr) spinach
1/4 cup butter
1/4 cup chopped onion
1   clove garlic, mashed
1/4 cup mashed basil
1   tablespoon unflavored gelatine
2   tablespoons water
3½   oz (100 gr) pistachio nuts, shelled
3/4 cup whipping cream
       salt and pepper, to taste
1   egg white

Wash and trim the spinach; cut off the stems and cook the spinach leaves 5 minutes in a tightly covered saucepan, without adding water. Cool and squeeze out the excess water, pressing between palms. Saute the onion, garlic, and basil in the butter until the onion is transparent. Dissolve the gelatine in the water. In a food processor, blend the onion mixture, gelatin, pistachios, and cream until the spinach is finely chopped and mixed with the other ingredients. In a separate bowl, beat the egg white into a soft meringue and fold into the spinach mixture. Grease a 6 inch (15 cm) heart-shaped pan with corn oil and pour the mousse into it; refrigerate overnight. Unmold onto a platter and garnish with a cucumber fan, carrot rolls and parsley sprigs. Serve cold.

Preparation time 12 hours

Feta Cheese in Phyllo

1   lb (500 gr) phyllo sheets
14   oz (400 gr) grated feta cheese
2   cups (200 gr) grated mild kefalotiri cheese
1   cup melted butter

Mix the two grated cheeses in a bowl. Lay a sheet of phyllo on the worktop and brush with melted butter.Sprinkle with the cheeses and a little water. Lay a second sheet of phyllo on top. Repeat, laying three sheets at a time. From the long side, roll up as a jelly roll. Make more rolls the same way, until all the phyllo sheets are used up. Wrap each roll separately in plastic wrap and freeze. When needed, remove one or two, and thaw slightly for 10 minutes. Cut into 1½ inch (3-4 cm) pieces and arrange on a buttered baking sheet with the cut ends up. Bake in a 350°F (175°C) oven for about 30 minutes, until golden brown. Serve hot.

Preparation time 1 hour

Pasta alle Vongole

2   lbs (1 kg) shrimp
1/2 lb (250 gr) squid
1   lb (500 gr) mussels, shelled
8   small clams
3   cups fresh or canned chopped ripe tomatoes
1   tablespoon tomato paste
1/2 cup dry white wine
1/2 cup water
1/2 cup olive oil
1   medium onion, sliced in rings
2-3 cloves of garlic
1   tablespoon finely chopped parsley or basil
1   tablespoon finely chopped mint
     salt and pepper, to taste
10   oz (300 gr) medium spaghetti

Clean the shrimp and the squid. Cut the squid into rings; wash and drain in a colander. Wash and scrub the clams under running cold water. Pull out and clip the beards with a scissors. Put the water and wine in a pot and bring to a boil. Add clams and shrimp and blanch for 1 minute. Drain and reserve the liquid. Wash and drain the mussels; wipe dry with paper towels. Heat the oil in a saucepan and saute

the onion and garlic. Remove with slotted spoon and set aside. Add the squid and saute until the liquid is absorbed and only the oil remains. Add the tomatoes, tomato paste, the sauteed onion, garlic, and the reserved liquid in which the shrimp and clams were cooked. Stir and simmer until the squid are tender and the sauce is thick. Add the shrimp, clams, mussels, parsley, mint, salt, and pepper. Boil the sauce for 5 minutes over high heat, stirring lightly. Remove from the heat. Bring half a large pot of water to a boil with 1 tablespoon olive oil. Add the spaghetti and cook for 8 minutes. Drain and toss with the sauce. Serve immediately.

Preparation time 1 hour and
30 minutes

Salmon Steaks in Wine

8   salmon steaks
1   cup dry white wine
1/3   cup lemon juice
3   tablespoons butter, in pats
1/2   cup finely chopped parsley
      salt and white pepper
1/4   cup whipping cream (optional)

Sprinkle the salmon with the salt and white pepper, cover and refrigerate for 30 minutes. Place the steaks in the center of a large shallow baking pan lined with heavy-duty aluminum foil, cut slightly larger than the pan. Pour the wine and lemon juice over them. Put 2-3 pats of butter on each steak and sprinkle with the chopped parsley. Bring the edges of the foil together so they completely cover the steaks, double-folding the edges so the salmon is sealed in. Bake in a 425°F (220°C) oven for 15 minutes. Remove from the oven, make an opening in one corner of the foil, and strain the juice through a fine sieve into a bowl. In a small saucepan, saute 1 tablespoon flour in 1 tablespoon butter over low heat for 1-2 minutes. Stirring constantly, add the strained juice and stir until the sauce thickens. Remove from the heat and adjust the seasoning. Add the cream, and stir over low heat until heated through. Pour the sauce over the salmon or serve separately in a sauce boat. Serve the fish with creamed potatoes and steamed vegetables such as asparagus, carrots, or zucchini.

Preparation time 1 hour

Fillet of Sole with Avocado Sauce

8   fillets of sole
     salt and pepper, to taste
1/2 cup white wine
2   tablespoons butter, in pats
2   egg yolks
4   tablespoons whipping cream
1   ripe avocado
1   tablespoon lemon juice
1/4 cup finely chopped parsley

Put the sole fillets in a buttered baking dish. Sprinkle with salt and pepper and pour the wine over the fillets. Put several pats of butter on each fillet and broil for 5 minutes. To prepare the sauce, blend the avocado with the lemon juice, salt, pepper and the parsley in a food processor until smooth. In a double boiler, combine the yolks with the cream and beat with a wire whisk until thick. Add the pureed avocado and continue stirring with the whisk until smooth and heated through. Arrange the fillets on a heated platter. Put a tablespoon of sauce on each fillet and serve with creamed potatoes and sauteed vegetables.

Preparation time 45 minutes

Creamed New Potatoes

1½   lbs (800 gr) new potatoes
2   tablespoons butter
2   tablespoons finely chopped green onion
4   tablespoons finely chopped parsley or dill
1   tablespoon finely chopped mint
2   teaspoons green pepper corns
1/2 cup mayonnaise
1   tablespoon lemon juice
1/2 cup whipping cream
     salt and pepper, to taste

Peel and cook the new potatoes in slightly salted water to cover; drain. If new potatoes are not available, cut round balls from large potatoes with a special potato cutter. Lightly saute the onion in the butter, and stir in the remaining ingredients; mix and heat thoroughly. Combine the cooked potatoes with the hot sauce and cook on low heat for 5 minutes. Otherwise, arrange the hot drained potatoes on a platter and pour the sauce over. Serve at once.

Preparation time 45 minutes

Aniseed Bread Rolls

Prepare bread dough as in the recipe, "Festive Bread" (page 163), substituting 2 teaspoons aniseed for 1 cup of the walnuts. After it has risen once, punch down the dough and divide into 19 equal pieces. Shape each piece into a smooth ball. Lay balls, smooth side up, 1 inch apart on a buttered 12 inch (30 cm) round baking pan. Place 12 balls around the outer edge of the pan, 6 on the inner edge and

one in the center. Cover with oiled plastic wrap and allow to rise in a warm place until doubled in bulk. Brush with egg yolk and sprinkle with onion seeds, sesame seeds and paprika. Bake in a 400°F (200°C) oven for 20 minutes, until well-browned.

Preparation time 2 hours and 30 minutes

Mixed Salad in Glass

7   oz (200 gr) green beans, cut in pieces
2   medium tomatoes, thinly sliced
5   green onions, sliced in rounds
1   small cucumber, sliced
10   large fresh mushrooms, sliced
2   avocados, cut into bite-sized pieces
1/4 cup finely chopped parsley

Cook the beans in boiling water 15-20 minutes until tender. Drain and set aside to cool. In a large footed glass salad bowl, put the green beans and lay the sliced tomatoes over them. Add the sliced green onions and continue with layers of cucumber, mushrooms, and avocado, sprinkling parsley in between. Garnish the top with a flower cut from fresh red pepper and onion. Cover with plastic wrap and refrigerate. Shortly before serving, dress the salad with one of the following dressings:

Garlic Dressing: In a small jar shake $1/3$ cup olive oil, 1 grated clove of garlic, 3 tablespoons vinegar, 1 tablespoon lemon juice, $1/2$ teaspoon sugar, 1 teaspoon mustard powder, $1/2$ teaspoon salt, and $1/8$ teaspoon freshly ground black pepper.

Mayonnaise Dressing: Mix 1 cup mayonnaise with 3 tablespoons sour cream, 2 teaspoons prepared mustard, 1 tablespoon lemon juice, a little salt and pepper. Thin with a little milk if too thick.

Preparation time 45 minutes

Banana Mousse

3   egg yolks
1/2   cup sugar
1/4   cup milk
1   cup mashed banana
2   teaspoons unflavored gelatin
1/4   cup water
3-4   oz (100 gr) white chocolate, melted
2   cups whipping cream
1   cup strawberry sauce
6   whole strawberries
1   oz (28 gr) semi-sweet chocolate, melted

Lightly grease a 5-cup heart-shaped mold with corn oil. Beat the yolks with the sugar until thick and creamy. Scald the milk in a saucepan and slowly pour into the egg mixture, beating continuously. Return to the saucepan and, stirring continuously, cook over low heat until the mixture thickens slightly, to cover the spoon. Take off the heat and stir in the mashed bananas. Soak the gelatin in the water until it swells; stir over low heat until dissolved. Add the gelatin and the melted chocolate to the bananas and stir until

thoroughly mixed. Chill until slightly thickened. Whip the cream into soft peaks. Reserve $1/3$ of it for the garnish and fold the remaining into the mousse. Turn into the prepared mold and refrigerate at least 4 hours. To serve, unmold on a platter and garnish with a garland of whipped cream rosettes around the edge and the 6 fresh strawberries dipped in the melted chocolate. The mousse should be served with strawberry sauce made as in the recipe, "Raspberry Cheese Cake"(page 55), substituting strawberries for the raspberries.

Preparation time 1 hour (refrigeration time not included)

Tiramisu

1   cup whipping cream
3   tablespoons powdered sugar
1   teaspoon vanilla extract
1   lb (500 gr) mascarpone or cream cheese
4   egg yolks
3   egg whites
1/3   cup sugar

2/3   cup espresso coffee
2/3   cup amaretto liqueur
11   oz (300 gr) ladyfingers
2   oz (50 gr) cocoa powder

Whip the cream, sugar, and vanilla until the mixture holds soft peaks. In another bowl, beat the cheese until light; continue beating while adding the yolks, one at a time. Beat the whites until foamy; adding the sugar a little at a time, continue beating until the mixture holds stiff peaks. Gently fold into the cheese mixture, first the whipped cream, and then, the meringue, taking care not to "deflate". In a small bowl combine the coffee with the liqueur. Briefly dip the ladyfingers, one at a time, in the liqueur and place side by side on the bottom of a 9-inch (22-cm) springform pan. Spread half the cream on top. Make another layer with the remaining ladyfingers and cream. Chill until firm and remove the ring. Sift the cocoa over the top. The word "Tiramisu" or other design may be stenciled with powdered sugar on the cocoa. Refrigerate uncovered, until ready to serve.

Preparation time 45 minutes (refrigeration time is not included)

Rice Pudding with Apricot Sauce

1½   cups water
2/3   cup short-grain rice
4   cups hot milk
2/3   cup sugar
7   oz (200 gr) white chocolate or chips
1   teaspoon vanilla
1   tablespoon unflavored gelatin
2   tablespoons water
1/4   cup chopped dried or candied apricots
1/4   cup chopped candied orange peel
1/4   cup white raisins
1¼   cups heavy cream, lightly whipped

Grease a 6-cup cake mold with corn oil. Put the water in a saucepan and bring to a boil. Stir in the rice, cover and lower the heat. Simmer until all the water has been absorbed. Add the hot milk and the sugar; continue simmering until the rice is soft, about 20 minutes. Remove from the heat. Add the vanilla and the chocolate; stir until melted and well-blended with the rice. Set aside to cool. Dissolve the gelatine in 2 tablespoons water and stir into the rice mixture; add the dried fruits, raisins and the lightly whipped cream; mix thoroughly. Pour into the oiled mold and refrigerate overnight. To serve, unmold the pudding on a platter, garnish with sliced orange halves and pour the apricot sauce on top.
Apricot Sauce: Combine 1 cup apricot juice with 1 tablespoon sugar and 1 tablespoon cornstarch dissolved in 2 tablespoons water. Simmer until the sauce is thick and clear. Remove from the heat, stir in 1 tablespoon of apricot liqueur.

Preparation time 1 hour and 30 minutes (refrigeration time is not included)

Organizing Mother's Day Menu

May, the heart of Spring, month of flowers and Mother's Day. This year, don't just send her flowers. Express your love by organizing a feast on her special day. Fill the house with flowers. Cook something exceptional, set out your best china and silver, and invite the rest of the family, with her as the guest of honor. Make a banana mousse in the shape of a heart to symbolize your love. Select a dry white wine to accompny the meal and a sweet Champagne for the desserts.
❀ *Each recipe serves 8 persons.*
❀ *Well in advance, prepare the feta rolled in phyllo and the aniseed rolls and freeze.*
❀ *Two days in advance, prepare the dessert of your choice, either the banana mousse, the rice pudding or the tiramisu.*
❀ *The day before, prepare the mixed salad and dressing and refrigerate separately. Prepare the spinach mousse and refrigerate.*
❀ *In the morning, prepare the seafood sauce. (Pasta will be cooked shortly before serving). Also, prepare the creamed potatoes and the steamed vegetables.*
❀ *One hour before, bake the feta rolls. Bake the salmon or sole and prepare the sauce; keep hot in a low oven or you may reheat in microwave.*
❀ *10 minutes before, cook the spaghetti, reheat the potatoes and vegetables, arrange on a platter with the fish and serve.*

Congratulations

MENU

Smoked Eel Pâté
Anchovy Pâté or Smoked Mussel Pâté
Potato and Meat Croquettes

❧

Carbonara

❧

Pork Tenderloin Wrapped in Caul
Saffron Rice Croquettes
Fried Apples

❧

Potpourri Salad with Blue Cheese Dressing

❧

Torte Timbale or Box of Roses Torte
Caramelized Oranges

❧

Cabernet Sauvignon or Merlot Wine
Sweet Champagne

Potato and Meat Croquettes

1   *lb (500 gr) potatoes*
1/2 *cup whipping cream*
1   *lb (450 gr) ground beef*
1/4 *cup grated Parmesan cheese*
1   *cup grated Romano or Parmesan cheese*
3-4 *oz (100 gr) cream cheese*
1/2 *cup grated onion sauteed in*
2   *tablespoons of butter*
1/8 *teaspoon grated nutmeg*
1/4 *teaspoon allspice*
1   *teaspoon herbs of Provence*
      salt and pepper, to taste
3   *egg yolks*

The Coating
3   *egg whites beaten with*
2   *tablespoons olive oil*
2   *cups crushed corn flakes*
      flour for dusting

Peel and cut the potatoes in large pieces. Half cover with water and cook until all the water is absorbed. Mash while gradually adding the cream; add the next 11 ingredients,

and combine well. Chill until stiff enough to form bite-sized balls. Roll them in flour, dip in egg white, and dredge in corn flakes. Butter a baking sheet and arrange the croquettes side by side. Freeze until firm; seal in plastic bags. They will keep several months. To serve, arrange again on a buttered baking sheet and bake in a 400°F (200°C) oven for 15-20 minutes until well browned. Serve hot.

Preparation time 1 hour and 30 minutes

Melba Toast Points

You can easily prepare your own thin crunchy toast points to accompany the various pâtés. They will keep for months in an airtight tin. Remove the crust from all sides of an unsliced loaf of white toast bread. Cut the bread loaf diagonally into two triangular pieces. Place on a bread board with the largest side down and using an electric knife, slice as thinly as possible. Arrange side by side on an unbuttered baking sheet and bake in a moderate oven 350°F (175°C) for 20 minutes or until they are lightly browned and completely dry. Cool before storing in a cookie tin.

Preparation time 40 minutes

Smoked Mussel Pâté

1   can of smoked mussels, 8 oz (250 gr)
7   oz (200 gr) cream cheese
1   tablespoon whipping cream
1   tablespoon mayonnaise
1   teaspoon lemon juice
1   teaspoon mashed fresh dill or fresh basil
1/2   teaspoon Worcestershire sauce
1   tablespoon sherry
    salt and white pepper, to taste

Reserve 4 whole mussels for the garnish. Put the remaining mussels in the food processor and blend until smooth. Add the rest of the ingredients and process until smooth. Cover and refrigerate overnight. To serve, put in a small shallow bowl and garnish with the whole mussels and sprigs of fresh dill.

Preparation time 5 minutes

Anchovy Pâté

4   oz (120 gr) anchovy fillets
1/4   cup mayonnaise
1   cup whipped cream
1   teaspoon unflavored gelatine dissolved in
2   tablespoons water
    salt and pepper, to taste

The Garnish
2   tablespoons finely chopped celery
2   tablespoons finely chopped firm tomatoes
2   tablespoons finely chopped black olives
1   tablespoon finely chopped fresh red pepper
1   tablespoon finely chopped fresh green pepper
2   tablespoons finely chopped green onions

In a food processor, puree the anchovies. Add the next 5 ingredients and process several seconds until the mixture is thick and smooth. Empty into a shallow bowl, cover with plastic wrap and refrigerate. Mix the chopped vegetables and garnish the pate shortly before serving.

Preparation time 15 minutes

Smoked Eel Pâté

3-4   oz (100 gr) smoked eel
7   oz (200 gr) cream cheese
1½   tablespoons lemon juice
1   tablespoon whipping cream
    salt and white pepper, to taste

In a food processor, blend the ingredients together into a thick smooth paste.Turn into a small shallow bowl and garnish with lemon slices and carrot strip bows.Alternatively, cut a cucumber into $3/4$ inch (2-cm) slices, scoop out the seeds, and with a pastry bag fitted with a large star tip fill the centers with pate. Cut little handles from pimento and place on top so they resemble small baskets.

Preparation time 5 minutes

Brioche

4   cups bread flour
1   teaspoon dry yeast or 1 oz (30 gr) compressed
1 1/4   teaspoon salt
1   tablespoon sugar
2/3   cup hot milk, 100°F (40°C)
2   tablespoons melted butter
1   egg plus 2 yolks
1/2   cup cold butter or margarine, in pats
1   egg yolk beaten with 1 teaspoon of water

Dissolve the yeast in the milk and set aside until foamy, about 10 minutes. Put the flour in a large bowl and make a well in the center.Put in the yeast and the rest of the ingredients except for the cold butter. Gradually pull in the flour from around the sides of the well, adding extra flour, if necessary, and knead to make a pliable, non-sticky dough. While lightly kneading the dough, add the butter a few pats at a time, and fold the dough over it. Continue until all the butter has been incorporated and the dough is smooth and elastic. Cover, and allow to rise in a warm place, until doubled in bulk, about 2 hours. Punch down and divide the dough into 24 golf ball-sized rolls, and the same number marble-sized balls. With your thumb make a deep depression in the centers of the large balls and place the small balls into them, wetting the ends to stick. Put the brioches in muffin tins, cover and allow to rise in a warm place, until doubled in bulk. Brush with the egg yolk and bake in a 350°F (180°C) oven for 15-20 minutes, until the tops are golden brown.

Glaze: In a small bowl, mix 1 tablespoon sugar,1teaspoon unflavored gelatin, and 2 tablespoons hot water. Stir over low heat until dissolved and brush the tops of the brioche immediately after removing them from the oven, to make them glossy.

Preparation time 3 hours

Potpourri Salad

2   bunches of rocket
2   large tomatoes, cut into bite size pieces
2   cucumbers cut into rounds
2   bunches of purslane

The Garnish
1   small cucumber cut into rings
2   onions, flower shaped
2   radish, rosettes

Wash the rocket and cut off the tender tops. Drain well and lay on the bottom of a glass salad bowl. Arrange the tomatoes on top and then the cucumber rounds. Carefully wash the purslane; choose the tender tops and arrange on top of the cucumber. Garnish with the cucumber rings, the onion and radish flowers. Cover with plastic wrap and refrigerate. Shortly before serving, dress the salad with olive oil and vinegar in 2 to 1 proportions, blended with a pinch of mustard, salt and black pepper; or serve with blue cheese dressing.

Preparation time 1 hour and 30 minutes

Blue Cheese Dressing

2   tablespoons wine or balsamic vinegar
2   tablespoons lemon juice
2   oz (50 gr) blue cheese
3   tablespoons whipping cream
1/2 cup olive oil

In a blender process the vinegar, lemon juice, blue cheese, and cream until well blended. Remove the cap and slowly add the olive oil in a thin stream, processing until the mixture is smooth and creamy.

Pork Tenderloin Wrapped in Caul

1   pork tenderloin, 3 lbs (1½ kg)
2   tablespoons softened butter
    salt and pepper, to taste

The Ground Meat Mixture
4   tablespoons butter
4   green onions, finely chopped
14 oz (400 gr) canned mushrooms, finely chopped
1/4 cup finely chopped celery
2   teaspoons cracked green peppercorns
2   teaspoons herbs of Provence
1/4 cup coarsely grated pistachio nuts
1/2 lb (250 gr) lean ground beef
1   lb (250 gr) ground pork
1   egg
1   large lamb caul
1   cup Madeira wine
1   cup beef stock
1   tablespoon corn starch

Salt and pepper the two pork fillets and spread with the softened butter. Bake in a 475°F (250°C) oven for 5 minutes. Remove from the oven and set aside. Meanwhile, prepare the ground meat mixture; saute the onion and mushrooms in the butter until wilted. Add the green peppercorns, herbs and the pistachios. Slightly cool the mixture; combine it with the two ground meats, the egg, and freshly ground black pepper, to taste. Cut the caul into two equal pieces. Lay one piece out on the worktop and spread it with half the meat mixture, enough to completely cover one fillet. Place the fillet in the center and picking up the edges of the caul, encase the fillet in the meat mixture. Tie securely with cotton string and repeat the procedure with the other fillet, caul and the remaining meat mixture. Place the rolls in the roasting pan with the remaining fillet juices. Bake rolls in a 400°F (200°C) oven for 20 minutes or until the caul is lightly browned. Remove from the pan and set aside. Add the wine to the roasting pan and scrape with a spatula to loosen the residue stuck to the bottom. Strain and refrigerate this broth for several hours. Scrape off all but 2 tablespoons of the solidified fat and discard the rest. Dissolve the cornstarch in a little cold broth and mix with the rest. Add the beef stock and simmer until the gravy thickens; adjust the seasoning. Cut the string off the fillet and slice. Serve hot accompanied by rice croquettes and fried apple. Pass the gravy in a heated gravy boat.

Preparation time 1 hour and 30 minutes

Saffron Rice Croquettes

2   tablespoons butter
3   tablespoons finely grated onion
2   cups water
1   cup short-grain rice
    salt and white pepper
1/8 teaspoon nutmeg
2-3 saffron stigmas, powdered
1   egg slightly beaten
1/2 cup grated Parmesan or kefalotiri cheese
1/2 lb (250 gr) cubed Gruyere, Gouda or mozzarella cheese
1   cup dry bread crumbs

In a large saucepan, saute the onion in the butter. Add the water, salt, and pepper, and bring to a boil; stir in the rice, saffron, and nutmeg. Cover and simmer until all the water has been absorbed. Remove from the heat, place 2-3 paper towels between the cover and the top of the pan and allow the rice to swell. When the rice is completely cool, mix with the egg and kefalotiri. Refrigerate overnight. The next morning, flatten a tablespoon of the cold rice mixture slightly in your palm and put a cheese cube in the center. Press the rice around it, forming a small ball. Roll the rice balls in the dry bread crumbs. At this stage, the croquettes may be frozen until needed. Shortly before serving, deep fry in hot oil, turning until browned on all sides. Drain on paper towels and serve immediately.

Preparation time 1 hour and 15 minutes

Carbonara

11	oz (300 gr) noodles (fettuccine) or medium spaghetti
2	tablespoons olive oil
	salt and pepper, to taste
2	tablespoons melted butter
5	oz (150 gr) lean bacon
3	egg yolks or 1 egg plus 1 yolk
1/2	cup whipping cream or evaporated milk
1/2	cup grated Parmesan or kefalotiri cheese
	extra grated Parmesan or kefalotiri cheese

Bring half a large pot of water to a boil with the oil and salt. Add the pasta and cook 8-10 minutes, taking care not to overcook. Meanwhile, cut the bacon in narrow strips and fry, over low heat until crisp. Drain on paper towels and discard all but 2 tablespoons of the fat. Stir in the yolks, Parmesan and freshly ground black pepper into the cream. Drain the pasta, return to the pot and toss with the butter, bacon and cream. Stir gently over low heat for 1 minute. Turn out onto a heated platter and serve immediately, sprinkled with the extra Parmesan or kefalotiri cheese.

Preparation time 20 minutes

Caramelized Oranges

8	medium oranges
1½	cups sugar
1½	cups water
2½	cups lemon juice
3	tablespoons Grand Marnier

With a peel stripper, pull off thin strips from the orange peel. Blanch them in water to cover for 10 minutes and drain. Clean the oranges, completely removing any orange or white parts of the peel. Cut each orange horizontally into 4 slices, for easy serving. Pass a wooden skewer through the center of the oranges to keep their shape, and place them in a deep glass bowl. Melt the sugar in the water over high heat and cook, until the syrup reaches the soft ball stage; add the blanched orange peel and simmer until glazed and transparent. Remove with a slotted spoon onto a buttered plate. Continue boiling the syrup until it is lightly caramelized; remove from the heat and stir in 1/4 cup water, to dissolve the caramel. If necessary, return to low heat to dissolve completely. Cool the syrup. Add the lemon juice, Grand Marnier and the orange peel. Pour over the oranges.

Cover with plastic wrap and refrigerate overnight.To serve, place the oranges in sherbert glasses or ice cream bowls, remove the wooden skewers, pour the syrup on top and garnish with the candied peel.

Preparation time 12 hours

Fried Apples

4   sour green cooking apples
lemon juice
clarified butter for frying
white pepper and grated nutmeg or cinnamon

Pare and core the apples. Slice in rounds ¼ inch (0.5 cm) thick and sprinkle with lemon juice to prevent discoloration; pat dry with paper towels before frying. Heat the butter in a frying pan on high heat and fry the apple slices until evenly browned on both sides. Remove to a heated platter, sprinkle with white pepper, nutmeg or cinnamon and serve immediately.

Preparation time 20 minutes

Organizing Congratulations Dinner

A promotion or achievement in the family is always cause for celebration, a time to share in the joy of our loved ones' success. It is usual to honor him or her with a gift of flowers or sweets. But have you thought of giving a "sweet bouquet" of pink marzipan roses? You may need to expend a little extra trouble and time, but dare to try making the "Box of Roses Torte" the next time you celebrate that "special achievement'" in the family. The satisfaction you will gain surely will exceed that which you offer. Prepare this festive menu and accompany with a good red wine such as Cabernet or Merlot and choose a sweet Champagne for the dessert.
❧ *Each recipe serves 8 persons.*
❧ *Well in advance, prepare the potato and meat croquettes, the rice croquettes, and the brioche. Store in Freezer.*
❧ *Three days in advance, make the pâtés and the melba toast.*
❧ *The day before, fix the torte of your choice, Timbale or Box of Roses Torte. Refrigerate.*
❧ *The evening before, prepare the caramelized oranges. Clean and cut all the vegetables are needed for the salad and prepare the dressing. Refrigerate separately. Set the table.*
❧ *During the day, prepare and roast the pork fillet. Take the brioche out of the freezer.*
❧ *Shortly before serving, fry both kinds of croquettes and the apples.*

Torte Timbale

1 ready-made sponge cake, 12 inches (30 cm) in diameter
4 tablespoons brandy
4 tablespoons maraschino or other liqueur
4 tablespoons milk
2½ cups whipping cream
1/3 cup powdered sugar
1 teaspoon vanilla extract
2/3 cup blanched, toasted almonds, coarsely grated
2/3 cup coarsely grated hazel nuts
7 oz (200 gr) semi-sweet baking chocolate

Slice the sponge cake horizontally in half. Line a deep metal bowl 8 inches (20 cm) in diameter with cheesecloth. (Or use a round salad or mixing bowl). Cut one of the slices into 16 wedges and place on the sides of the bowl with the tips meeting in the center. Arrange the pieces alternately with browned tops and cut bottoms toward the outside. Combine the brandy, milk, and liqueur, and sprinkle 2/3 of it on the cake. Whip the cream with the powdered sugar and the vanilla until stiff and divide in half. Melt half the chocolate and cut the other half into small pieces. Carefully stir the cooled melted chocolate and half the nuts into one part of cream. Fold the chocolate pieces and the other half of nuts

into the rest of cream. Refrigerate both cream mixtures until stiff. Spread the dark mixture on the surface of the cake lining the bowl. Refrigerate briefly until firm and then fill the center space with the white cream mixture. Trim the second sponge slice to fit the top, and sprinkle with the rest of the brandy mixture. Cover with plastic wrap and refrigerate overnight. Shortly before serving, unmold on a platter, carefully pull off the cheesecloth and sprinkle with a little powdered sugar and cocoa.

Preparation time 2 hours

Box of Roses Torte

The Pastry
2 cups all purpose flour
1/4 teaspoon salt
3/4 cup butter
4½ tablespoons water

The Filling
2 cups heavy cream whipped with
1/2 cup powdered sugar and 1 teaspoon vanilla extract
28 oz (800 gr) canned cherries
2 tablespoons sugar
2 tablespoons cornstarch
1/8 teaspoon almond extract

The Garnish

1/4 cup raspberry or strawberry jam
1/4 recipe Rolled Fondant (page 112) or
1/2 lb ready-made Rolled Fondant (Regalice)
1/2 recipe Almond Paste (page 184)
  red and green food colorig

The Pastry: Prepare the pastry as in the recipe, "Chocolate Tart"(page 88). Roll it out thinly between two sheets of waxed paper into a rectangular 15x16 inch (38x40 cm) sheet. Remove waxed paper from the top and cut crosswise into three equal pieces with a sharp knife. Move the divided dough carefully with the bottom waxed paper onto a large baking sheet. Pierce the dough all over with a fork. Bake in a 400 °F (200 °C) oven for about 20 minutes or until lightly browned. Cool and separate the pieces along the cut lines.

The Filling: Drain the cherries and thicken the juice with the sugar and cornstarch in a saucepan over low heat; cool slightly. Stir in the almond extract and the cherries. Set aside. Put the chilled whipped cream in a pastry bag fitted with a large plain tip.

Assembling the Torte: Place one of the tart pieces in the bottom of a florist's box. Starting at one edge, pipe strips of whipped cream down the length of the tart 1/2 inch (1 cm) apart, ending at the opposite edge. In between the whipped cream strips, carefully place strips of cherries, one next to the other. Place the second tart piece on top and repeat, putting strips of whipped cream and cherries down its length. Spread one side of the third tart piece with the marmalade and carefully place it on the torte (marmalade side facing up).

To Garnish: Tint the Rolled Fondant pink with a few drops of red coloring and roll it out into a rectangle to fit on top of the torte. Place it over the top. Color half the almond paste pink and the other half green. Roll each out to a 1/8 inch (.003 cm) thickness. Cut out leaves with a special leaf cutter or make a pattern from cardboard. Press a pattern of veins into the leaves with a wooden skewer or toothpick. Roll very thin strings for the stems or use a tube of purchased green glaze. For the roses, cut large and small ovals. Shape one into a cone. Holding it at its base, place three other "petals" around the cone, turning them out to form the rose in full bloom. Use two smaller ovals to make rose buds. For the base of the roses, cut small star shapes from the green paste; wrap and pinch them around the base of the rose. Place the roses and leaves along the stems to create a lifelike bouquet of roses. The preparation time for this torte depends entirely on your dexterity but your effort will surely rate many kudos from those present.

FATHER'S DAY CELEBRATION

MENU

Eggplant and Mozzarella Fritters

❧

Macaroni Timbale Surprise

❧

Duckling à l'Orange
Broccoli Mousse
Onions à la Crème

❧

Endive and Spinach Salad
Cheese Board

❧

Apple Soufflé or Peach Pudding
Cheesecake Roll

❧

Ruby Cabernet Wine

Endive and Spinach Salad

1	lb (450 gr) tender curly endive
1	lb (450 gr) young short-stemmed spinach
1/4	cup coarsely grated walnuts
3	slices of white bread, without crusts and cubed
2	tablespoons butter
	a bit of grated garlic
4	tablespoons grated kefalotiri cheese
4	tablespoons vinegar
6	tablespoons olive oil
	salt and pepper, to taste

Wash and trim the endive and the spinach, discarding the large tough outer leaves; cut the tender leaves in small pieces. Set aside in a colander, to drain well. In a small frying pan, briefly saute the garlic in the butter; remove and discard the garlic. Coat the cubed bread with the butter, spread out on a baking sheet and toast them in a 340°F (175°C) oven, until golden brown. When ready to serve, layer the greens in a glass salad bowl with croutons and walnuts in between. Sprinkle the salad with the cheese and dress with 1/2 cup of salad cream or vinaigrette dressing. Toss just before serving.

Preparation time 30 minutes

Eggplant and Mozzarella Fritters

2	large round eggplants
1/2	lb (250 gr) mozzarella, thinly sliced
1	tablespoon finely chopped fresh basil
	salt and pepper, to taste
	corn oil for frying

The Batter

1/2	cup flour
	salt and pepper, to taste
1	tablespoon olive oil
1/2	cup beer or soda water
1	egg white

Completely peel the eggplant and slice into rounds 1/4 inch (0.5 cm) thick. Sprinkle with a little salt on both sides and set aside for 1 hour. Beat together all the batter ingredients except for the egg white and set aside for 1 hour. Rinse and drain the eggplant thoroughly, pressing them between your palms. Lightly saute in hot oil and drain on paper towels. Sprinkle with salt, pepper, and the basil. Sandwich a slice of cheese between two slices of eggplant. At this stage they may be frozen. Beat the white to a soft meringue and fold into the batter. Dip the eggplant "sandwiches" into the batter, allowing the excess to run off. Fry in hot oil a few at a time until browned. Drain well on paper towels. Serve hot or cold with salad cream. To make the salad cream: Mix $^1/_2$ cup mayonnaise, $^1/_4$ cup strained yogurt, 1 teaspoon prepared mustard, $^1/_4$ teaspoon sugar, $^1/_2$ teaspoon finely grated onion, 1 tablespoon lemon juice, salt, and freshly ground pepper, to taste.

Preparation time 1 hour and 30 minutes

Macaroni Timbale Surprise

11	oz (300 gr) thick macaroni (ziti or mostaccioli)
2	tablespoons soft butter or margarine
1	tablespoon finely chopped parsley
2	eggs
1	cup grated stale bread
1/3	cup milk
1/4	cup whipping cream
2	tablespoons grated onion
12	oz (350 gr) ground cooked turkey or ham
	salt and pepper, to taste
1/2	lb (250 gr) frozen spinach
3/4	cup cream cheese
1	egg
2/3	cup whipping cream
2	tablespoons flour
	pinch of grated nutmeg
1½	cups grated Swiss cheese or Grùyere

Cook the macaroni 10 minutes in salted water with 1 tablespoon oil. Drain and lay the strands out on absorbent paper, so they are not touching each other. With your fingers, spread the butter over the entire inside surface of a 9-cup round metal bowl. Sprinkle with the parsley. Starting from the bottom center, wind the strands of macaroni in a spiral completely covering the entire inside surface of the bowl, up to the top. Cover and refrigerate. Meanwhile, cut the remaining macaroni into $^3/_4$ inch (2 cm) pieces. In a food processor, mix the eggs, bread, milk, cream, onion, salt, and pepper. Add the ground turkey or ham and process at medium speed for 3 minutes. Carefully spread and pat the mixture evenly on top of the macaroni lining the bowl. Cover and chill. Blanch the spinach and drain well. Squeeze between your palms to remove the excess water. Set aside. Beat the cream cheese with the egg until smooth; continue beating, while gradually adding the cream, flour, nutmeg, salt, and pepper. Stir in the spinach, the chopped macaroni and the grated cheese. Fill the center space of the bowl with this mixture. Cover with aluminum foil, leaving a small opening in the center. Place in a baking pan containing $^1/_2$ inch (1 cm) of hot water. Bake in a 350 °F (180 °C) oven, for 1 hour and 30 minutes or until firm. Remove from the oven and take out of the water; cool for 15 minutes before unmolding on a platter. Garnish with parsley and sliced tomato.

Preparation time 2 hours and 30 minutes

Organizing your Father's Day Celebration

A salute to Father, a day dedicated to the one who looks after us the other 364 days of the year. He deserves an extra-special dinner in his honor, prepared with exceptional care. Begin the meal with a macaroni timbale surprise. Then present him with the elegant Duck à l'Orange, an exceptionally fragrant and tasty entrée. Garnish a platter of his favorite cheeses with a gondola filled with fruit. Choose his favorite red wine to accompany the meal. And last, but not least, choose one of the three desserts, any of which is sure to please. A special note for your table setting are the napkins folded like tuxedos, complete with velvet bow ties, in keeping with the occasion.

❧ *Each recipe serves 8 persons.*

❧ *Well in advance, prepare the macaroni timbale, the dinner rolls, peel the onions, and store in the freezer.*

❧ *The day before, fix the eggplant fritters without frying them. Prepare the salad and the cheesecake roll, if it's your choice for dessert.*

❧ *The evening before, stuff the duck and refrigerate. Set the table. Take the macaroni timbale out of the freezer. Prepare the cheese platter.*

❧ *In the morning, prepare the broccoli mousse, and the onions with the sauce. Remove the rolls from the freezer.*

❧ *Four hours in advance, bake the macaroni. When it is done, put in the duck to roast. Prepare the pudding or the soufflé, whichever your choice, and put in the oven after taking out the duck. Fry the eggplant fritters.*

❧ *Shortly before the duck is ready, heat the macaroni over steam, unmold and serve.*

Duckling à l'Orange

5-6 lbs (2½ kg) frozen duck

The Stuffing

1/4 cup toasted, coarsely ground almonds
2 tablespoons butter or margarine
1/4 cup grated onion
1/4 cup finely sliced mushrooms
1/2 lb (250 gr) ground beef
1 ' tablespoon finely chopped celery
1/3 cup rice, half white, half wild rice
    salt and pepper, to taste
1/2 cup coarsely chopped sour apple

The Glaze

1/2 cup beef or chicken stock
1/2 cup orange juice
3 tablespoons light brown sugar
1/4 teaspoon ground ginger

The Gravy

3 tablespoons light brown sugar
1/4 cup red wine vinegar
1 cup beef or chicken stock
    cornstarch for thickening
2 tablespoons port wine
1 tablespoons lemon juice

The Garnish

    caramelized orange roses
    shoe string potatoes

Draw the duck as soon as it has defrosted. Boil the neck and giblets for use in making the glaze, if desired. Pluck the pin feathers with a tweezers and singe the bird, if necessary. Prick the skin of the duck all over with a pointed metal skewer. Drain and rub the inside with salt and pepper. The Stuffing: Saute the onion in the butter until transparent. Add the mushrooms and the ground meat and cook until all the liquid has been absorbed. Remove from the heat and add the remaining stuffing ingredients. Mix well and adjust the seasoning. Lightly stuff the neck cavity. Draw the skin over the back and secure with wooden skewers or truss with a string. Stuff the stomach cavity with the rest of the filling and secure with skewers or sew shut. Tie the legs close to the body. Place on a rack in a large roasting pan and roast uncovered in a 350°F (175°C) oven, for 2 hours or until the skin is well browned. The Glaze: Combine the glaze ingredients and cook for 1 minute. Take the duck out of the oven and carefully remove the skewers or strings. Increase the oven temperature to 400°F (200°C). Brush the duck with the glaze and continue roasting for 30 minutes, basting several times with the glaze until the skin is shiny and crisp. Remove the stuffing. Place the duck on a platter, surround with the stuffing and shoestring potatoes; keep warm. Strain the juices from the roasting pan to a saucepan; skim off and discard all but two tablespoons of the fat. Reserve this liquid for the gravy. The Gravy: In a small saucepan, boil the brown sugar and the vinegar until a thick caramel syrup is formed. Add the reserved pan juices and stir over low heat to dissolve the caramel. Stir in the stock and 1 or 2 teaspoons cornstarch dissolved in cold water. Cook until thick and transparent. Remove from the heat, add 1-2 tablespoons port wine and 1 tablespoon lemon juice. Serve the gravy in a sauce boat.

Preparation time 3 hours and 30 minutes

Bacon-Flavored Dinner Rolls

Prepare bread dough as in the recipe for "Whole Wheat Rolls" (page 87). With a scissors, finely cut ¹/₂ lb (250 gr) of bacon. Fry over medium heat, stirring often until crisp. Remove with a slotted spoon and drain on paper towels. Roll out the dough into a rectangle 8x16 inches (20x40 cm). Sprinkle the bacon over the entire surface. Starting from the long edge, roll up tightly. Cut into 1¹/₄ inch (3 cm) pieces and arrange, cut edges down, on a baking sheet. Cover and let rise in a warm place until doubled in bulk. Bake in a 400°F (200°C) oven, for 15 minutes. Cool and store in airtight plastic bags in the freezer until ready to use.

Broccoli Mousse

2   lbs (1 kg) broccoli, washed and trimmed
1¹/₂ teaspoon salt
4   eggs, slightly beaten
1/4   cup whipping cream
1/4   teaspoon nutmeg
1/4   teaspoon pepper
1   tablespoon soft butter

In a large pot, cook the broccoli in salted water until tender, about 15 minutes. Drain and cool. Cut into pieces and puree in a food processor. In a bowl, combine the puree with the eggs, cream, salt, pepper, and nutmeg. Butter a 4-cup metal bowl or ring mold. Pour the broccoli mixture into it and cover with aluminum foil. Put the mold in an ovenproof dish with 1-inch (3-cm) of hot water and bake in a 350°F (180°C) oven for about 30 minutes or until the blade of a knife inserted into the mousse comes out clean. Unmold on a platter and serve with creamed onions.

Preparation time 1 hour

Onions à la Crème

30   small dry onions, peeled
4   tablespoons butter
4   tablespoons all purpose flour
       salt and white pepper, to taste
1/8   teaspoon grated nutmeg
2   cups hot milk
1/2   cup whipping cream

Cook the onions in salted water until soft, about 50 minutes. Drain and set aside. In a saucepan, melt the butter and stir in the flour, salt, pepper, and nutmeg. Continue stirring while cooking over low heat for 2 minutes. Remove from the heat and slowly stir in the hot milk and the cream. Return to heat, continue stirring until the sauce is thick and smooth. Add the onions and carefully stir until they are heated through. Remove from the heat, cover with plastic wrap stuck on the surface and set aside to cool. Refrigerate until ready to use. To reheat, add a little water or milk and gently stir over low heat. Serve hot with the broccoli mousse.

Preparation time 1 hour

Apple Soufflé

2	tablespoons butter or margarine
4	medium cooking apples
1/3	cup sugar
2	tablespoons lemon juice
4	eggs, separated
3	teaspoons cornstarch
1/2	cup whipping cream
1	teaspoon lemon zest
1	teaspoon vanilla extract
1/4	cup sugar
	icing sugar for the topping

Peel and core the apples; slice 7 thin uniform rounds,

sprinkle with lemon juice, and set aside.Thinly slice the rest of the apples, lengthwise. In a heavy-bottomed frying pan, melt half the butter. Stir in half the sugar and half the lemon juice. Add the sliced apples.Toss in the sugar mixture, and simmer until nearly all the juice has been absorbed.Turn into a round buttered 10-inch (25-cm) baking dish and spread evenly on the bottom. Beat the yolks with the mixer, until thick; add the cornstarch, cream, lemon zest, and the vanilla. Beat until light. In another bowl, whip the whites until foamy. Adding the rest of the sugar a little at a time, continue beating into a soft meringue. Fold the meringue into the yolk mixture and spread over the apples. In the same frying pan, heat the remaining butter, sugar and lemon juice. Saute the apple rounds in the mixture, until the liquid has been absorbed and the apples are glazed. Arrange them symmetrically on top of the soufflé and bake in a 350°F (180°C) oven, for about 30 minutes. Top with a little powdered sugar and serve immediately.

Preparation time 1 hour and 15 minutes

Peach Pudding

12	oz (800 gr) canned peaches or apricots
3	cups milk
1	cup whipping cream
5	cups cubed sliced bread, lightly toasted
1	cup chopped pitted prunes
8	egg yolks
1/3	cup sugar
1/4	teaspoon salt
1	lemon (juice and zest)
1/4	teaspoon ground nutmeg
4	tablespoons melted butter
4	egg whites
	pinch of cream of tartar
1/2	cup sugar

Drain the canned peaches. Reserve the juice and set aside the fruit. Simmer the juice until reduced to a thick syrup and combine with the milk, bread, and prunes. Beat the egg yolks with the sugar, cream, lemon juice, zest, salt, and the nutmeg. Combine with the bread mixture. Stir in the melted butter. Turn out into a buttered 10-inch (25-cm) ovenproof dish. Place in a pan with hot water and bake in a 350°F (180°C) oven for about 50 minutes. Meanwhile, beat the egg whites with the sugar and cream of tartar into a stiff meringue. Spread evenly on top of the hot pudding, forming peaks with the back of a wooden spoon. Return to the oven for 15 minutes, until the meringue is lightly browned. Serve the pudding while still warm, accompanied by the peaches or peach sauce made as in the recipe for "Cherry Sauce" (page 175). Slice the peaches before using for the sauce.

Preparation time 1 hour and 15 minutes

Cheese Board

Arrange a variety Dad's favorite cheeses attractively on a wooden cheese board or tray. Garnish the cheeses and the tray with various fresh seasonal fruits. Carve a gondola from a large cucumber and fill it with fresh fruits, vegetables, pickles, and olives. Place it in the center of the cheese board.

Cheesecake Roll

The Filling
11   oz (300 gr) softened cream cheese
1/2   cup sugar
1   egg plus 1 yolk
1½   tablespoons whipping cream
1   teaspoon orange zest

The Cake
1/2   cup self-rising flour
1/4   teaspoon salt
4   eggs, separated
1   teaspoon vanilla extract
2/3   cup sugar
2   oz (60 gr) semi-sweet baking chocolate, melted

The Garnish
powdered sugar
caramelized orange peel
caramelized orange peel roses (page 70)
chocolate sauce (page 165)

Line a jelly roll pan 10x15 inches (25x38 cm) with lightly buttered baking paper. Beat the cream cheese with the sugar. Add the egg, yolk, milk, and orange zest. Beat until smooth and creamy. Spread the mixture evenly on the paper. To prepare the cake, sift the flour with the salt. Beat the yolks with the vanilla and 1/3 of the sugar, until thick and creamy. Stir in the cooled melted chocolate. In a separate bowl, beat the egg whites until thick. Continuously beating, gradually add the remaining sugar and whip until the meringue holds soft peaks. Fold half the meringue into the yolk mixture. Sift the flour on top and fold in. Then, gently fold in the other half of the meringue, taking care not to deflate. Put the cake mixture into a pastry bag fitted with a large plain tip and pipe it evenly onto the cheese mixture. Bake in a 400°F (200°C) oven for about 15 minutes until it tests done with a toothpick. Turn out onto a kitchen towel sprinkled with powdered sugar and carefully peel off the paper. Starting at the short edge, roll up, jelly roll fashion. Cool and place on an oblong cake plate. Dribble a little chocolate sauce over the top and garnish with caramelized orange peel and orange peel roses.

Preparation time 1 hour

$\mathcal{S}$UPPER BY THE SEASIDE

<u>MENU</u>

Blue Cheese Spread or
Crabmeat Rolled in Cheese

❧

Clam Chowder

❧

Peppered Beef Tenderloin
Baked Potatoes

❧

Avocado Salad

❧

Honey Dinner Rolls

❧

Fruit Platter
Chocolate Cream Tart
Strawberry Torte

❧

California Port and Cabernet Wine

Blue Cheese Spread

8	oz (228 gr)	Roquefort or blue cheese
8	oz (228 gr)	cream cheese
2	tablespoons	mayonnaise
1	tablespoon	sour cream or strained yogurt
5	drops of	Tabasco sauce
5	drops	chili sauce
3-4	oz (100 gr)	pistachio nuts, chopped

Put all the ingredients except for the nuts in a food processor and blend. Chill until stiff enough to form a ball. Roll in chopped pistachio nuts. Cover with plastic wrap and refrigerate 8-12 hours. Serve with crackers or melba toast and thin slices of carrot.

Preparation time 15 minutes

Crabmeat Rolled in Cheese

1	cup	ketchup
1	tablespoon	chili sauce
15	drops of	Tabasco sauce
14	oz (400 gr)	cream cheese
1	tablespoon	whipping cream
9	oz (250 gr)	cooked crabmeat, flaked

Combine the first 3 ingredients into a smooth sauce. In another bowl, soften the cheese with the whipping cream. Spread on a piece of aluminum foil into a rectangle 8x12 inches (20x30 cm). Spread the crabmeat lengthwise down the center with a two or three tablespoons of sauce. Lift the sides of the foil and bring towards the center, encasing the crabmeat in the cream cheese. Refrigerate 2-3 hours. Turn out onto a platter and carefully remove the foil. Garnish with crabmeat pieces and parsley. Put a little sauce in a pastry bag and dribble some over the top. Serve the remainder in a bowl.

Preparation time 15 minutes

Peppered Beef Tenderloin

4-5	lbs (2.5 kg)	beef tenderloin
10	teaspoons	green peppercorns, crushed
4	teaspoons	coarsely crushed black pepper
10	tablespoons	clarified butter
8	tablespoons	brandy
1	cup	beef stock
1	cup	whipping cream
2	teaspoons	extra green peppercorns
		salt

Slice the tenderloin into 10 steaks. Press $1/2$ teaspoon of the

green peppercorns onto each side and work them into the meat with the flat side of a cleaver or mallet. Sprinkle with the black pepper. Divide the butter into two large frying pans and melt over high heat. Fry five steaks in each pan for 3 minutes on each side, until done on the outside, and rare and juicy on the inside. Drain most of the butter from the pan and discard. Put 4 tablespoons of brandy in each pan, take off the heat and light. When the flame extinguishes itself, remove steaks to a heated platter and keep warm. Add the stock to one pan, scraping the bottom with a wooden spatula, and pour into the other pan. Add the cream, extra green peppercorns, and salt, to taste. Simmer while stirring the sauce, until it thickens. Pour over the steaks and serve hot with sauteed vegetables and baked potatoes.

Preparation time 30 minutes

Clam Chowder

36	clams
4	tablespoons butter
1	cup grated onion
2	tablespoons flour
2½	cups water
14	oz (400 gr) potatoes, peeled and diced
1/4	teaspoon white pepper

3/4	cup whipping cream or milk
4	tablespoons finely chopped parsley

Scrub the clams with a stiff brush under running water until clean and free of sand. Rinse well and put in a pot with 2 cups of water. Simmer on low heat until they open. Drain and strain the liquid through cheesecloth. Open the clams and cut the meat from the shell. In a large pot, heat the butter and saute the onions until transparent. Stir in the flour and cook for one minute. Add the clam liquid, the water, the potatoes, the salt, and pepper. Simmer until the potatoes are soft. Meanwhile, chop the clam meat and add to the soup along with the whipping cream. Stir over low heat until heated through, taking care not to boil. Serve sprinkled with chopped parsley.

Preparation time 30 minutes

Avocado Salad

2   *ripe avocados*
2   *tablespoons lemon juice*
1   *red bell pepper, cut into strips*
1   *yellow bell pepper, cut into strips*
    a few purslane tops
    small head of leaf lettuce
1   *stalk of celery, thinly sliced*

The Dressing

1/2 *cup olive oil*
2   *tablespoons ground walnuts*
1   *small clove of garlic, mashed*
1   *egg*
2   *tablespoons vinegar*
1   *tablespoon lemon juice*
1/4 *teaspoon Worcestershire sauce*
    a few drops of Tabasco sauce
    salt and pepper, to taste

The Dressing: Put the olive oil, ground walnuts and mashed garlic in a jar, shake well and allow to stand for 1 hour. Put the egg in boiling water for 1 minute. Strain the seasoned oil and discard the walnuts and garlic. Break the egg into a blender and process until blended. Remove the blender cap and continue blending while slowly adding the oil in a thin steady stream; without stopping the blender, add the vinegar, the lemon juice, Worcestershire sauce, Tabasco sauce, salt and pepper. Refrigerate until ready to use. Meanwhile peel and remove pit from the avocado. Slice into strips and sprinkle with lemon juice. Combine avocado with the other salad vegetables in a serving bowl, cover with plastic wrap, and refrigerate. Pour the dressing over the salad just before serving.

Preparation time 20 minutes

Baked Potatoes

10   *large uniform-sized potatoes*
1/2 *cup finely chopped green onion or chives*
1/4 *cup finely chopped parsley*
2   *cups sour cream*

Scrub well and rinse the potatoes under running water; pat dry with paper towels. Wrap each one in aluminum foil and put in a 400 °F (200 °C) oven. Bake for 1 hour and 30 minutes or until soft. Combine the onion and parsley in a small bowl. With a sharp knife, slash the potatoes crosswise and press them to open. Serve with the sour cream sprinkled with the onion parsley mixture.

Preparation time 1 hour and 45 minutes

Honey Dinner Rolls

4   cups whole wheat flour
1½   cups bread flour
1½   tablespoons active dry yeast or
1½   oz (45 gr) fresh compressed yeast
3   tablespoons honey
3   tablespoons olive oil
2   teaspoons salt
1   egg (optional)
1½   cups warm water 100°F (40°C)

Combine both the flours with the dry yeast in a large basin and open a well in the center. If using fresh yeast, dissolve in half a cup of the warm water and set aside until foamy. Pour in the sugar, oil, egg, and water. Gradually incorporate the flour from the sides of the well into the liquid and knead adding extra flour as needed, until dough is smooth and elastic, about 15 minutes. Cover and set aside in a warm place to rise until doubled in bulk, about 2 hours. Punch down, and divide the dough into 2 oz (50 gr) pieces, about the size of a golf ball. Arrange well apart on a baking sheet, cover, and allow to rise. Sprinkle the surface with flour and make two parallel slashes with a razor blade on the surface of the rolls. Bake in a 350°F (180°C) oven for 20-30 minutes. Cool on a rack. Freeze in an airtight plastic bag, until ready to use.

Preparation time 3 hours

Fruit Platter

Choose two perfect melons of the same size. On the surface of one, sketch a swan and on the other, a duck. With a sharp knife cut through the melon along this outline, removing the unnecessary portions. With a melon baller, cut small round balls of melon, peach, mango, apple, or whatever fruit is in season. Arrange the fruits inside the two melons and place them on a platter surrounded by more fruits including sliced kiwi, orange and tangerine sections, strawberries and cherries.

Preparation time 1 hour

Chocolate Cream Tart

The Pastry

1$^1/_3$	cups all purpose flour
1/8	teaspoons salt
1/2	cup cold butter, cut into pieces
3	tablespoons cold water

The Filling

5	oz (150 gr) semi-sweet baking chocolate or chips
2	tablespoons butter
3	tablespoons cocoa
2	tablespoons evaporated milk
2	eggs, separated
1/2	teaspoon lemon zest or a few drops of almond extract
1	cup heavy cream, whipped
1/2	cup powdered sugar
1/2	cup blanched almonds, finely chopped and toasted maraschino cherries and whipped cream for the garnish

Combine the flour and salt in a bowl. Cut the butter into the flour with a pastry blender or with your fingers, until it resembles coarse breadcrumbs. Sprinkle with the cold water and gently work, until the mixture holds together in a ball. Do not knead or overwork the dough or it will toughen. On a floured surface, roll out the pastry into a 11-inch (28 cm) circle and ease it into a 10-inch (25-cm) tart dish, so that the bottom and sides are covered. Flute the edges with your fingers. Prick the crust with a fork and bake in a 400 °F (200 °C) oven for 15-20 minutes, until lightly browned. Set aside to cool. For the filling, combine the chocolate, butter, cocoa, and milk in a heavy-bottomed pan on low heat and stir until the chocolate has melted and the mixture is blended. Cool and add the two egg yolks and the lemon zest. Gently fold in the whipped cream. Beat the egg whites with the sugar into a soft meringue and fold into the chocolate mixture. Carefully stir in the toasted almonds. Pour into the cooled crust and refrigerate until set. Garnish with maraschino cherries and whipped cream.

Preparation time 1 hour

Strawberry Torte

5	egg whites
1/2	teaspoon cream of tartar
1$^1/_4$	cups sugar
1/2	teaspoon vanilla
3/4	cup ground toasted almonds or hazelnuts
7	oz (200 gr) semi-sweet chocolate bits
1/4	cup milk
2$^1/_2$	cups heavy cream, whipped
1/4	cup powdered sugar

1	teaspoon vanilla
1	lb (500 gr) fresh strawberries, washed and hulled; reserve 9 perfect ones with stems for garnish
1/2	recipe caramel candy (page 26)

Beat the egg whites with the cream of tartar until thick and foamy. Beating continuously, gradually add the sugar and vanilla. Continue beating until the meringue holds soft peaks. Carefully fold in the almonds or hazelnuts. Draw two circles 9 inches (23 cm) in diameter on baking paper. Divide the meringue in two parts and spread half on each circle, completely covering the surface. Bake the meringues on racks in a 340 °F (175 °C) oven for 35-40 minutes. Melt the chocolate in a heavy-bottomed pan over low heat. Dip the bottom halves of the reserved strawberries in the chocolate. Drain the excess and put on a plate; refrigerate to set. Stir the milk into the remaining chocolate, blend well and cool. Place one meringue base on a platter and spread with half the chocolate. Spread a thick layer of whipped cream over the chocolate and cover the entire surface with strawberry- halves. Spread the remaining chocolate on the second meringue base and place it on top of the strawberries (the chocolated part facing the strawberries). Cover the entire torte with whipped cream. Arrange the chocolated strawberries evenly around the torte. Insert abstract caramel "spikes" randomly between the strawberries. To make them, prepare half a recipe of caramel candy and dribble the hot caramel on a lightly buttered marble or ceramic surface, forming modernistic spikes or sticks. Refrigerate the torte until ready to serve.

Preparation time 3 hours

Organizing your Supper by the Seaside

This simple, easy to prepare menu of classic regional American specialties is an ideal way to entertain guests at your beach house. Begin the meal with a tasty clam chowder. Serve the pepper steak with a choice red wine. End with a luscious chocolate cream tart for dessert. Reveal your artistic abilities by creating the melon swans filled with a selection of fresh fruits of the season. Serve port wine with the appetizers and a full-bodied red wine as Cabernet or Pinot Noir with the Peppered Beef Tenderloin.

❀ *Each recipe serves 10 persons.*
❀ *Two days in advance, prepare the rolls and the tart. Freeze the rolls and store the tart in the refrigerator.*
❀ *The day before, make the blue cheese or crabmeat spread. Scrub and wrap the potatoes in aluminum foil.*
❀ *In the morning, prepare the soup and saute a few carrots and zucchini. Prepare the fruit platter.*
❀ *In the afternoon, fix the avocado salad and the dressing. Chill in the refrigerator.*
❀ *Two hours in advance, bake the potatoes and fry the steaks.*

ENGAGEMENT PARTY

<u>MENU</u>

Smoked Trout Mousse

❧

Farfalle with Salmon and Caviar

❧

Poached Salmon with Green Sauce
Sauteed Vegetables

❧

Jellied Salad

❧

Watermelon Galley
Meringue Fruit Tart or
Mint Filled Chocolate Tarts

❧

White Burgundy Wine and
Sweet Champagne

Smoked Trout Mousse

8	oz (225 gr) smoked trout
1	tablespoon finely chopped green onion
1	tablespoon finely chopped dill
3	tablespoons each finely chopped red, yellow, and green pepper
	salt and pepper
4	tablespoons mayonnaise
1	tablespoon lemon juice
1	tablespoon gelatin
1/4	cup water
1	cup whipping cream, lightly beaten
	tender lettuce leaves, thinly sliced lemon rounds, red caviar, and
	carrot rosettes for the garnish

Mash the trout and combine with the onion, dill, peppers, salt, and pepper. Add the mayonnaise and lemon juice and mix well. Sprinkle the gelatin on the water and dissolve over low heat. Set aside to cool. Stir the cream and the cooled gelatin into the trout mixture and mix gently. Grease two 1½-cup molds with corn oil; divide the mousse evenly into the molds. Use heart or clover-leaf shaped molds, or any other available. Chill in the refrigerator until set, preferably one day in advance. Unmold onto a bed of lettuce leaves and garnish with sliced lemon, red caviar and carrot rosettes. Cover with plastic wrap and refrigerate until ready to serve.

Preparation time 4 hours

Jellied Salad

1	cucumber, thinly sliced
1	large carrot, thinly sliced
1	lb (450 gr) seedless green grapes
1½	cups water
1	package lemon gelatin
3	tablespoons orange juice
5	tablespoons lemon juice
1	tablespoon finely grated onion
1/8	teaspoon cayenne pepper
1/2	teaspoon salt
1/4	teaspoon pepper

The Marinade

6	tablespoons olive oil
2	tablespoons good quality wine vinegar

1/4   teaspoon salt
1/4   teaspoon pepper
1/4   teaspoon powdered mustard

Cut the grapes in half. Mix the ingredients for the marinade together. In separate bowls, pour 1/3 of the marinade over the grapes, 1/3 over the cucumbers, and 1/3 over the carrots. Marinate for 30 minutes, mixing every so often. Boil 3/4 cup water and dissolve the gelatin in it. Add the remaining water, the orange juice, the lemon juice, the onion, salt, cayenne and freshly ground black pepper. Strain 1/2 cup of the gelatin through a fine sieve and pour into a 5-cup ring mold. Chill in the refrigerator until set but not firm. Meanwhile, return the remaining solids in the strainer to the rest of the gelatin. Arrange a circle of overlapping cucumber slices on the set gelatin in the mold. Carefully pour another 1/2 cup of gelatin over that and return the mold to the refrigerator for 10 minutes. Meanwhile, strain the grapes and the carrots. Stir 4 tablespoons of the marinade into the remaining gelatin. Chill until it begins to thicken, 5-6 minutes. Mix the grapes into the thickened gelatin and pour carefully over the cucumbers in the mold. Arrange the sliced carrots around the outer rim of the mold pressing lightly into the gelatin. Cover with plastic wrap and refrigerate overnight. To unmold, place the mold in warm water for 10 seconds. Shake gently to loosen and unmold on a round platter. Garnish with a bunch of parsley.

Preparation time 12 hours

Organizing your Engagement Party

The betrothal of two young people is perhaps one of the most meaningful and important days as they celebrate their decision to join their futures. Prepare a festive dinner for this important occasion. Fold the napkins into fans and hold together with lemon leaves and blossoms in silver ring holders. An arrangement of white lilies and baby's breath with two white candles make a breathtaking centerpiece for the table. Serve this menu of discreet flavors and tastes with a white Burgundy wine. For the fruit tart, open a bottle of sparkling Champagne.

❀ *Each recipe serves 10 persons.*

❀ *One month in advance, prepare the rolls and freeze. Also, prepare the meringue base for the fruit tart. Cover with plastic wrap and keep in a dry place.*

❀ *Two days in advance, prepare the trout mousse and refrigerate in the molds. Also, prepare the chocolate tartlets and the jellied salad.*

❀ *The day before, make the fruit tart and fill the tartlets with the mint mousse. Prepare all the ingredients for whatever will be cooked the next day.*

❀ *In the morning, take the rolls out of the freezer. Saute the vegetables which will be served with the salmon. Unmold and garnish the trout mousse and the jellied salad. Prepare the watermelon galley and fill it with fruit. Prepare the sauce for the salmon and also prepare the salmon steaks for poaching. Refrigerate.*

❀ *Shortly before sitting down, prepare the pasta farfalle.*

❀ *Before serving place the salmon in the oven.*

Poached Salmon with Green Sauce

3	14 oz (400 gr) cans of baby artichokes
1	14 oz (400 gr) can of asparagus
4	large carrots
10	salmon steaks
1/4	cup olive oil
	salt and white pepper
1/3	cup butter
1/3	cup margarine
1	tablespoon lemon juice

The Sauce

2	tablespoons butter
2	tablespoons flour
2	cups fish stock
1/4	cup whipping cream
4	tablespoons herbed butter prepared with
4	sprigs each of dill and parsley and
1	thin green onion

Drain the artichokes and the asparagus. Peel and slice the carrots into rounds. Cook in slightly salted water until tender. Drain and set aside. Brush the salmon steaks with the oil and sprinkle with salt and white pepper. Cover and refrigerate for 30 minutes. Meanwhile, prepare the garnish.

Heat half the butter and half the margarine in a small saucepan over medium heat and saute the artichokes and carrots. Saute the asparagus in the remaining butter and margarine. Pour the lemon juice over the sauteed asparagus and keep all the vegetables warm. Arrange the salmon steaks on a rack over the broiler pan. Put 8 cups of boiling water in the pan and cover the salmon with heavy-duty aluminum foil, sealing it well around the rim of the pan. Put the pan in a 425 °F (220 °C) oven and poach the salmon for 15 minutes. Meanwhile, prepare the sauce. Melt the butter and saute the flour. Add the fish stock, stirring vigorously, and simmer the sauce until thick and smooth. Stir in the whipping cream. Heat just to the boiling point and remove from the heat. Add the herbed butter in pieces, stirring vigorously until blended. Arrange the salmon steaks and the vegetables on a silver platter and accompany with the sauce, served separately in a sauce boat.

To prepare the herbed butter: Blanch 4 sprigs of fresh dill, 4 sprigs of parsley and one green onion for 2-3 minutes. Strain and pat dry with paper towels. Mash with a fork and work in 4 tablespoons of softened butter until blended. Pass through a fine strainer with a spatula and discard the remaining coarse stems. Chill the herbed butter until ready to use.

Preparation time 1 hour

Gingered Dinner Rolls

1   recipe bread dough for Sesame Twists (page 150)
3   tablespoons butter or margarine, softened
2   teaspoons powdered ginger
1   egg yolk beaten with
1   teaspoon water
1/4 cup sesame seeds

Prepare the dough according to the recipe on page 150. After the first rising, punch down and divide the dough into three parts. On a lightly floured surface, roll out each piece into a rectangle 12x14 inches (30x35 cm). Spread the first sheet with half the softened butter, sprinkle with 1 teaspoon ginger, and cover with the second sheet. Spread with the rest of the butter and sprinkle with 1 teaspoon ginger. Cover with the third sheet of dough. Cover with a cloth and allow to rest for 10 minutes. Cut lengthwise into $\frac{1}{2}$ inch (1 cm) strips. Twist the strips, roll them into pinwheels, and arrange on a lightly buttered baking sheet allowing enough room for them to rise. Cover and allow to rise until doubled in bulk. Brush with the beaten egg yolk. Form a cone with a clean sheet of paper and cut a small opening at the tip. Fill the cone with sesame seeds and fill the depressions along the lines of the pinwheel. Bake in 400 °F (200 °C) oven 15-20 minutes, until browned.

Preparation time 3 hours

Farfalle with Salmon and Caviar

11   oz (300 gr) farfalle pasta
1½   cups evaporated milk
9   oz (250 gr) smoked salmon, chopped
9   oz (250 gr) smoked cheese
1/4   cup finely chopped parsley
      salt and pepper, to taste
1   small jar of black caviar
1   small jar of red caviar
      several sprigs of parsley and
1   smoked salmon "rose", for the garnish

Cook the pasta in boiling salted water with 2 tablespoons of salad oil for 8 minutes, or al dente. In a large non-stick pan, scald the milk, add the cheese and stir until melted. Stir in the salmon, parsley, salt, and pepper. Drain the pasta and gently fold into the cheese sauce. Turn out onto a deep platter or shallow glass bowl and garnish with the caviar and the sprigs of parsley. Shape a long strip of smoked salmon into a rose and place on top. Serve immediately.

Preparation time 45 minutes

Meringue Fruit Tart

The Meringue
3   tablespoons cocoa
1   cup fine sugar (not powdered)
1/2   teaspoon vanilla extract
4   egg whites
1/4   teaspoon cream of tartar

The Filling
4   oz (120 gr) white chocolate
1/2   cup milk
2   tablespoons butter
1   cup whipping cream
1/4   cup powdered sugar
1/2   teaspoon vanilla extract
4   kiwis, peeled and sliced
1   navel orange, sectioned
4   large strawberries
1   envelope quick-gel fruit gelatin.

Mix the cocoa with 1/3 cup of the sugar. Beat the egg whites with the cream of tartar and the vanilla in the mixer at high speed, until thick and fluffy. Continue beating while gradually adding the rest of the sugar until the meringue holds soft peaks. Add the cocoa mixed with sugar in 2-3 parts gently blending it into the meringue. Put the meringue in a pastry bag fitted with a large star tip and pipe a spiral 9 inches (22 cm) in diameter on a sheet of non-stick baking paper. Pipe large rosettes around the outer edge of the spiral. Bake the meringue on a rack in a very slow 200 °F (80-90 °C) oven (with the fan on, if you have a convection oven) for about 2 hours. Turn off and allow meringue to cool in the oven. Seal airtightly in plastic wrap and store in a dry place until ready to use.

The filling: Melt the chocolate in the milk in a heavy bottomed saucepan over low heat, stirring until smooth. Remove from the heat, stir in the butter and allow the mixture to cool. Whip the cream with the sugar and vanilla until stiff. Reserve 1/2 cup for the garnish. Fold the remaining cream into the cooled chocolate mixture. Spread the filling into the prepared meringue and refrigerate until set. Attractively arrange the fruits on the filling taking care not to let them touch the meringue. Glaze the fruits with the gelatin prepared according to the directions on the package. Garnish with whipped cream rosettes and refrigerate uncovered for a maximum of 24 hours.

Preparation time 2 hours and 30 minutes

Mint Filled Chocolate Tarts

The Tarts
11   oz (300 gr) semi-sweet baking chocolate or chips
2   tablespoons corn oil

The Filling

7	oz (200 gr) cream cheese, softened
1/2	cup powdered sugar
2	tablespoons crème de menthe liqueur
1	cup whipping cream
1/2	teaspoon vanilla extract
3-4	drops green food coloring

Stir the chocolate with the corn oil in a small heavy-bottomed saucepan over low heat until melted. Place 12 regular cupcake liners in a muffin tin. Use two liners together for extra support. Dip a pastry brush in the melted chocolate and completely coat the bottom and sides of the liners. Refrigerate until firm. Repeat, brushing melted chocolate, especially over any thin areas. Chill again until firm. Carefully peel off cupcake liners. Keep refrigerated. For the filling, beat the cream cheese with half the powdered sugar and the mint liqueur until smooth and light. In a separate bowl, whip the cream with the rest of sugar and the vanilla until thick, and fold into the cream cheese mixture. For a brighter green, add 2-3 drops of the food coloring. Divide the filling among the chocolate shells and refrigerate until set. Garnish with chocolate scrolls (made by scraping a two-colored chocolate bar with a potato peeler) and small heart-shaped chocolate cutouts. Keep refrigerated.

Preparation time 1 hour and 30 minutes

Watermelon Galley

A dessert of cool and aromatic fresh fruit is the best way to end a meal. Symbolically representing the life the young couple are about to embark on, this watermelon galley filled with fruits of the season is sure to delight everyone, both visually and gastronomically.

Preparation time 45 minutes

WEDDING RECEPTION

MENU

Spinach Rings
Pâté-Filled Oranges
Meat-Stuffed Eggplant Rolls
Fruit-Stuffed Pork Tenderloin
Mussels Stuffed with Rice
Sole Fillets in Aspic
Pimento Rolls with Cheese
Risotto Parmigiana
Artichokes Florentine
Stuffed Chicken Wings

Fresh Green Salad Platter
Mixed Cheese Appetizers

Mocha Torte
Chocolate Viennese Torte
Wedding Cake

A Variety of White and Red Wine,
Champagne

Bread Sticks

3   cups all purpose flour
3   tablespoons sugar
1   teaspoon aniseed (optional)
1   teaspoon salt
4   teaspoons baking powder
3/4   cup water
1/3   cup olive oil
1   tablespoon brandy
    sesame seeds

Place the first 5 ingredients in the mixing bowl. Add the oil, brandy, and the water. Beat with the mixer fitted with the dough hook on low speed, until the dough gathers around the dough hook. Scrape the dough off the hook into a bowl. Cover and allow to rest for 10 minutes. Roll out into a rectangle 8x16 inches (20x40 cm), and cut into $1/2$ inch (1 cm) strips lengthwise. Using a pastry brush, lightly wet with a little water and roll in sesame seeds. Alternatively, brush half the strips with egg yolk and sprinkle with coarse salt. Arrange the bread sticks on a baking sheet lined with non-stick baking paper and bake in a 400 °F (200 °C) oven for 5 minutes. Lower the temperature to 350 °F (175 °C) and bake for another 15 minutes. Cool on a rack. Store in an airtight container.

Preparation time 1 hour

Pâté-Filled Oranges

7   oz (200 gr) finely ground beef
3-4   oz (100 gr) finely ground pork
3-4   oz (100 gr) chicken livers
2   slices cooked ham
2   medium onions, grated
1   clove of garlic, mashed
3-4   oz (100 gr) pistachio nuts, coarsely chopped
1   tablespoon green peppercorns
1   egg
2   tablespoons sherry wine
2   tablespoons Grand Marnier
1/4   teaspoon ground coriander
1/8   tablespoon allspice
    salt and pepper
6   large oranges
6   slices of tomato

Ask your butcher to grind the beef and pork twice. Remove

the veins and membranes from the livers and mince in a food processor with the ham. Add the ground beef and pork, the onion, and the garlic; process until blended for 2-3 minutes. Empty into a bowl and mix in the remaining ingredients, salt, and freshly ground black pepper, to taste. Knead the mixture for a few minutes, cover and chill. Meanwhile, remove a slice from the top of each orange and scoop out the pulp. Sprinkle a little brandy into each orange and brush the exteriors with a little melted butter. Put a small piece of butter into each orange cup and place in a 350°F (180°C) oven until melted. Pierce the orange in several places with a skewer and fill with the pâté. Top each orange with a slice of tomato and arrange in an ovenproof dish. Bake in a 350°F (180°C) oven for 1 hour. Cool, cover and chill in the refrigerator for 24 hours. To serve, divide into 4 sections taking care not to separate the pieces and arrange on a bed of lettuce.

Preparation time 24 hours

Meat-Stuffed Eggplant Rolls

4½   lbs (2 kg) eggplants
1   lb (500 gr) ground beef
1/4   cup olive oil
1   large onion, grated
1/2   cup finely chopped parsley
3   tablespoons ketchup
2   tablespoons grated mild kefalotiri cheese
2   tablespoons grated Parmesan cheese
2   tablespoons dried breadcrumbs
      salt and pepper

The Sauce
3   tablespoons olive oil
1   clove garlic
1   small hot pepper
3   cups pureed fresh or canned tomatoes
1/2   teaspoon sugar

Peel the eggplant and cut into lengthwise slices, ¹/₄ inch (¹/₂ cm) thick. Salt and set aside for 1 hour. Rinse and squeeze to get rid of excess moisture. Lightly saute in olive oil and allow to cool on kitchen towels to absorb excess oil. Heat the olive oil and saute the onion until transparent. Remove from the heat, add the ground beef and the rest of the ingredients and knead the mixture for a few minutes until soft and pliable. Form 45 small meatballs. Set aside. Saute the garlic and pepper in the olive oil for 1-2 minutes, remove and discard. Add the tomatoes, sugar, salt and freshly ground pepper, cover and simmer for 30 minutes. Strain the sauce through a fine sieve. Spread the bottom of an ovenproof dish with several tablespoons of sauce. Roll the meatballs in the eggplant strips and place them side by side on the sauce. Pour the remaining sauce over them. They may be frozen at this stage. Bake in a 400°F (200°C) oven for about 40 minutes and serve hot.

Preparation time 2 hours

Organizing the Wedding Reception

A wedding reception at home has a friendly, personal character and costs much less than any other venue. However, it takes much preparation and proper organization. The recipes suggested here serve 20 persons, but they can be adapted to serve as many guests as your home can accommodate. If you have a large garden, hold the reception outside under the stars. Since this is dependent on the weather, be sure to have an alternative available. You will need plenty of dishes, glassware and silverware. Set up a bar in one corner and stock it with two or three kinds of wine, champagne, various apéritifs, as well as soft drinks. Hire specially trained personnel for the occasion and enlist the aid of friends and relatives to help you with the decorations and the cooking of the food that day. All the dishes suggested here can be prepared well in advance and stored in the freezer. Arrange tables set for 4-6 persons around a space where the guests can dance. Place special lanterns with candles around the garden and on the tables which will create a romantic setting for this very special occasion.

❀ *Well in advance, prepare the eggplant rolls, the spinach rings, the stuffed pork tenderloin, artichokes Florentine, the stuffed chicken wings, the cake bases and store them in the freezer.*

❀ *Three days in advance, prepare the Mocha torte, the Viennese torte, the wedding cake and the pâté-stuffed oranges and store in the refrigerator.*

❀ *Two days in advance, prepare the pimento rolls and the cheeses. Store in the refrigerator.*

❀ *The day before, prepare the jellied sole fillets and the stuffed mussels. Wash the salad greens.*

❀ *During the day, cook or bake all the frozen dishes.*

❀ *Shortly before serving, prepare the risotto.*

Fresh Green Salad Platter

Choose fresh tender seasonal vegetables and greens such as lettuce hearts, purslane, rocket, curly endive, tomatoes, cucumbers, carrots and green onions. Wash well and drain.

Cut in pieces or separate the leaves and arrange attractively on a platter. Cover tightly with plastic wrap until ready to serve. Sprinkle with salt and a little vinegar or lemon juice shortly before serving. The vegetables can be served also with two or three dressings in separate bowls next to the platter. Choose thick dressings, such as those with mayonnaise, yogurt, or Roquefort, more adaptable to buffet service. Serve cottage cheese or dressing made of cottage cheese and avocado for those who prefer something light.

Cottage Cheese Dip

11   oz (300 gr) cottage cheese
1   ripe avocado
1/2   cup grated Parmesan or kefalotiri cheese
1-2   tablespoons chili sauce
2   tablespoons lemon juice
      salt and pepper

Pulse all the ingredients in a food processor until smooth.

Preparation time 45 minutes

Spinach Rings

2   *lbs (1 kg) spinach, blanched and squeezed dry*
1   *cup grated Parmesan or Romano cheese*
2   *cups crumbled feta cheese*
3   *eggs*
1   *cup whipping cream*
1/8 *teaspoon grated nutmeg*
      salt and pepper, to taste
1   *lb (500 gr) phyllo*
1/2 *cup olive oil mixed with ¹/₂ cup melted margarine*
1   *egg yolk beaten with*
1   *teaspoon water*
2   *tablespoons onion seeds*

Combine the spinach with the cheese and the eggs. Add as much cream as needed to have a soft mixture. Add salt, freshly ground pepper, and the nutmeg; mix well. Cut the phyllo sheets in half crosswise. Butter each sheet, spoon 2 tablespoons of spinach filling along the long edge, and roll up. Bring the ends together to form a ring, wetting the ends with water to make them stick. Continue with the remaining filling and phyllo sheets. Arrange the rings on a buttered baking sheet and brush with the egg yolk mixture. Sprinkle with onion seeds. At this stage the spinach rings can be frozen. Bake at 350°F (180°C) for about 45 minutes, until browned. They are equally tasty, hot or cold.

Preparation time 1 hour and 30 minutes

Fruit-Stuffed Pork Tenderloin

4   *lbs (2 kg) pork tenderloin*
      salt and pepper
10 *large seedless dried prunes*
10 *dried apricots*
1/2 *cup clarified butter*
1/2 *cup dry white wine*
2/3 *cup orange juice*
2   *tablespoons lemon juice*

Cut the tenderloins down the middle lengthwise, taking care not to cut completely through. Open out and pound flat. Sprinkle half of them with salt and pepper and place the prunes lengthwise down the center. Lift the edges of the meat towards the center, forming a roll with the prunes in the middle. Secure the edges with wooden skewers or toothpicks. Repeat the same procedure with the other tenderloins placing the apricots in the center. In a large oval pan melt the butter and saute the rolls on each side. Add the wine, the orange and lemon juices. Cook the rolls in the simmering juice, basting and turning them several times, until the meat is tender, about 20 minutes. Remove the rolls and thicken the juice with a little cornstarch. Taste, and adjust the seasoning. Cut the rolls crosswise into thick pieces. Arrange on a platter and accompany with the orange sauce, served in a sauce boat.

Preparation time 1 hour and 30 minutes

Artichokes Florentine

24   *frozen artichoke bottoms*
1/3   *cup melted butter*
1/4   *cup lemon juice*
      salt and pepper, to taste
1   *lb (500 gr) spinach leaves (without stems)*
2   *tablespoons olive oil*
1   *small clove of garlic, mashed*
24   *large shrimp, cleaned and blanched*

   The Bechamel Sauce
2   *tablespoons butter*
2   *tablespoons flour*
2/3   *cup scalded milk*
1/3   *cup whipping cream*
1   *cup grated Parmesan or Romano cheese*
1/8   *teaspoon grated nutmeg*

Choose artichokes which are tender and not stringy. Arrange close together in a baking dish. Combine the butter with the lemon juice, salt, and pepper, and brush the artichokes with the mixture. Cover with aluminum foil and bake in a 400°F (200°C) oven until tender, about 40 minutes. Meanwhile, finely chop the spinach, blanch and drain. Squeeze out the excess moisture with your hands. Heat the oil in a saucepan with the garlic and saute the spinach over medium heat for a few minutes, stirring continuously.

Prepare the bechamel sauce: Melt the butter in a saucepan and saute the flour for 1 minute. Stirring vigorously, add the hot milk. If lumps form, pass through a sieve or buzz in a blender. Stir and cook until thick. Add the nutmeg, whipping cream, and grated cheese. Continue, to cook stirring until heated through. Add the sauteed spinach, stir, and remove from the heat. Add salt and freshly ground black pepper to taste. Remove the artichokes from the oven and place one shrimp in each. Spread two tablespoons spinach filling over the top. At this stage the stuffed artichokes can be frozen, or refrigerate until ready to use. Shortly before serving, bake in a 400°F (200°C) oven for 30 minutes or until they start to brown.

Preparation time 1 hour and 30 minutes

Stuffed Chicken Wings

30   chicken wings, about 4 lbs (2 kg)
1   lb (500 gr) shrimp or crabmeat
1/2   teaspoon sugar
1   teaspoon cornstarch
      salt and pepper
2   tablespoons corn oil
2   tablespoons finely chopped green onions
2   tablespoons finely chopped celery
2   tablespoons finely chopped carrot
4   eggs
1/4   cup milk
1/4   cup sesame
2   cups dried bread crumbs

Wash the chicken wings and pat dry with paper towels. Cut off the bottom joints. With a sharp knife, separate the meat from the bone and pull the meat and the skin inside out over the shoulder joint, forming a pocket. Another method, better but more difficult, is to leave the bottom joint of the wing attached. With a scissors cut the edge of the skin of the upper section and carefully remove the bones. This method allows a large space for the filling. Clean and devein the shrimp. Rinse and pat dry. Chop finely in a food processor and mix with the sugar, cornstarch, salt, and freshly ground pepper. Heat the oil in a small saucepan and saute the onion, carrot and the celery until soft. Combine with the shrimp mixture and bind with one of the egg whites. Fill each wing pocket with 1 teaspoon of the filling. Beat the eggs with the milk in a bowl and in a separate one combine the sesame seeds with the bread crumbs. Put some flour in a third bowl. Roll the wings in the flour, dip into the beatten egg mixture, and finally, roll in the bread crumbs, coating all sides. Refrigerate for 20 minutes so the coating will set. At this stage they may be frozen. Fry in medium hot oil until the center is cooked and the outside is browned. Serve hot. The wings can be fried in advance and heated in a hot oven shortly before serving. Serve with the following sauce: Combine 1 cup dark soy sauce, a bit of mashed garlic, 1/2 teaspoon grated ginger, 1 tablespoon sugar, and 1 tablespoon cornstarch. Simmer slowly while stirring until the sauce is thick and clear.

Preparation time 3 hours

Sole Fillets in Aspic

3   lbs (1½ kg) sole (4 large sole divided into 16 fillets)

The Fish Stock
the bones from the sole
1   carrot
1   stalk of celery
1   small onion
1   clove garlic
2   bay leaves
1   teaspoon peppercorns
3   cups water
1   cup dry white wine

The Filling
2   tablespoons lemon juice
    salt and white pepper
1   sweet red pepper, finely chopped
1   green pepper, finely chopped
1   cup finely chopped fresh dill
1   cup finely chopped parsley
2   tablespoons unflavored gelatin
1   teaspoon sugar
2   egg whites

Wash the bones. Put the bones in a saucepan with the rest of the stock ingredients, except for the wine. Bring to a boil over medium heat. Skim, cover and simmer for 40 minutes.

Add the wine and simmer for another 10 minutes. Set aside for 5 minutes and strain, discarding the solids. Rinse the sole fillets and drain well. Sprinkle with the lemon juice, salt, and white pepper. Combine the chopped peppers, dill, and parsley; spread a teaspoon of the mixture on the fillets. Sprinkle a little powdered gelatin on the filling and carefully roll up. Wrap each roll separately in aluminum foil. Arrange the rolls close together in a large pan and carefully cover with ample hot fish stock. Cover and simmer for 15 minutes. Remove from the heat and allow to cool in the stock. With a slotted spoon remove rolls from the stock. Carefully remove the foil and cut each roll in half with a sharp knife. Combine the remaining stock in a saucepan with the rest of gelatin, the sugar, salt, and white pepper. Beat the egg whites into a soft meringue and add to the stock. Stir over high heat until it starts to boil, remove from the heat and allow to cool for 10 minutes. Strain through a sieve lined with absorbent paper towels. Spoon 2-3 tablespoons of hot aspic into each of 30 custard cups and refrigerate until set. If you don't have enough cups, prepare the aspic in two parts. Place one fillet roll into each cup with the cut side down. Add enough hot aspic to cover. Chill for 4 hours until firmly jelled. Dip each cup quickly into hot water and unmold on a wet platter. Cover with plastic wrap and refrigerate until ready to serve.

Preparation time 4 hours

Mussels Stuffed with Rice

3   *lbs (1½ kg) fresh live mussels*
1/3 *cup olive oil*
1/2 *cup chopped onion*
1/2 *cup finely chopped green onion*
1¼ *cup long-grain rice*
1/2 *cup finely chopped dill*
     salt and pepper

Scrub the mussels with a stiff brush under running water. Debeard and put in a large pan with a cup of water over high heat until they open. Strain and reserve the liquid. Heat the oil in a large pan and saute the onions. Stir in the rice and saute for 1-2 minutes. Measure the reserved liquid, add enough hot water to make 3 cups, and pour it into the pan containing the rice. Add 2 teaspoons salt, the dill, and freshly ground pepper, to taste. Bring to a boil, cover and simmer the rice until tender, about 20 minutes. Shell the mussels and add them to the rice. Mix and cool slightly. Choose 40-50 of the larger mussel shells. Fill them with rice and at least one mussel. Arrange attractively on a round platter and place this on a larger tray of lettuce leaves. Garnish with a flower cut out from a red pepper. Cover with plastic wrap and refrigerate. Serve cold.

Preparation time 2 hours and 30 minutes

Pimento Rolls with Cheese

1   *large jar of pimentos*
3-4 *oz (100 gr) cream cheese*
3-4 *oz (100 gr) ricotta cheese*
3-4 *oz (100 gr) mild soft feta cheese*
3-4 *oz (100 gr) mascarpone cheese*
1   *small clove of garlic, mashed*
2   *tablespoons chopped parsley or mint*
     salt and pepper

Cut the peppers into long strips about 1.5 inches (4 cm) wide. With a fork, mash all the cheeses together and combine with the mashed garlic, parsley or mint, salt, and freshly ground pepper. Spread an ample quantity of the cheese mixture on each pimento strip and roll up. Arrange on a platter, cover with plastic wrap and refrigerate until served.

Preparation time 30 minutes

Mixed Cheese Appetizers

The Pine Cone
14	oz (400 gr)	cream cheese
8	oz (240 gr)	grated Cheddar cheese
3		tablespoons sherry or port wine
1/8		teaspoon cayenne pepper
1/4		cup finely chopped green onions

Variation
14	oz (400 gr)	cream cheese
4	oz (120 gr)	blue cheese, crumbled
4	oz (120 gr)	Swiss cheese, grated
2		tablespoons brandy
1		small clove of garlic, mashed
1/4		teaspoon white pepper

The Garnish
2	cups bacon-flavored salted almonds

The Carrot
3-4	oz (100 gr)	cream cheese
7	oz (200 gr)	Cheddar cheese, grated
1/2		cup chopped salted pistachios

1/4		cup grated carrot
2		tablespoons finely grated onion
1/8		teaspoon dried dill

For the pine cone, choose whichever version suits your taste. Combine and blend the ingredients in a food processor for 1-2 minutes until smooth. Cover and refrigerate until stiff. Shape the cheese mixture into a large "pine cone" and place on a cheese board. Starting at the tip of the cone, press the almonds carefully into the cheese mixture in rows, making sure that the pointed end of each almond extends at a slight angle. Continue pressing almonds into cheese mixture in rows, slightly overlapping, until the entire surface is covered. Garnish the top with pine sprigs. For the carrot, blend the two cheeses in a food processor. Blend in the rest of the ingredients and refrigerate until stiff. Form into the shape of a large "carrot"and shortly before serving, garnish the top with carrot tops or fresh dill sprigs. Keep refrigerated. Serve the cheese spreads with crackers and melba toast.

Preparation time 40 minutes

Bread Basket

Prepare rolls, either all the same, or choose two or three different kinds and shapes. Make them one or two months in advance and freeze. Remove from the freezer the morning of the reception and attractively arrange in bread baskets. Homemade rolls make an attractive addition to your wedding buffet and are sure to please your guests.

Preparation time 3 hours

Risotto Parmigiana

2   cups long-grain rice
1   cup Champagne
1   cup Parmesan cheese
    salt and pepper

Partially cook the rice with ample water. Strain and place in a large pan, over high heat. Pour in the Champagne and stir until the Champagne has been evaporated. Stir in the cheese, salt, and freshly ground black pepper. Serve immediately. For an unusual and outstanding presentation, serve the risotto in a hollowed-out head of Parmesan decorated with a large ribbon bow.

Preparation time 40 minutes

Mocha Torte

The Cake

1	cup softened unsalted butter
1½	cups sugar
1	teaspoon vanilla extract
6	eggs
2	cups self-rising flour
1/4	cup cornstarch
1/3	cup cocoa
1/3	cup milk
1/3	cup brandy
1	cup finely chopped toasted almonds

The Filling

1/2	cup custard powder
1/2	cup sugar
2	cups hot milk
2	tablespoons instant coffee
2	tablespoons water
1	cup softened unsalted butter
1/2	cup powdered sugar

The Glaze

4½	oz semi-sweet chocolate pieces

1/2   cup unsalted butter

Put the first 8 ingredients for the cake into the mixing bowl of an electric mixer and beat at medium speed for 4 minutes, until light and fluffy. Divide the mixture into two rectangular cake pans 10x15 inches (25x38 cm) lined with non-stick baking paper. Bake in a 350°F (175°C) oven for 30-35 minutes. Turn out the cakes onto waxed paper and allow to cool. Cut each cake crosswise into three rectangular pieces. Sprinkle with the brandy. In a saucepan, combine the custard powder and the sugar. Add the hot milk and stir vigorously over medium heat until the custard thickens. Press on the surface a sheet of plastic wrap, to prevent a crust from forming, and set aside to cool. Meanwhile, dissolve the coffee in the water. Cream the butter into the powdered sugar until fluffy. Gradually add the cooled custard and the coffee into the creamed butter and mix carefully. Reserve 1 cup of the cream and divide the rest into 5 equal portions. On a platter, stack the cake layers one on top of the other, spreading the cream in between. Melt the chocolate with the butter in a double boiler and set aside to cool. Beat with a wooden spoon until thick and spread on the top surface of the torte. Frost the sides with the reserved filling and press the toasted almonds around the torte. Put some filling into a pastry bag fitted with a plain narrow tip and pipe parallel lines 1-inch (2-cm) apart, lengthwise on the chocolate surface of the torte. With a wooden skewer drow crosswise lines 1-inch (2-cm) apart, perpendicular to the piped ones, pulling the skewer alternately down and then up, for a feathered effect. Cover with plastic wrap and refrigerate.

Preparation time 2 hours

Chocolate Viennese Torte

8	*egg whites*
1	*cup sugar*
1/2	*teaspoon cream of tartar or*
1	*tablespoon lemon juice*
1	*teaspoon vanilla extract*
2½	*cups, 11 oz (300 gr) finely chopped almonds (with the skin)*
21	*oz (600 gr) semi-sweet baking chocolate or chips*
4	*tablespoons corn oil*
2½	*cups whipping cream*
1/2	*cup powdered sugar*

1   *teaspoon vanilla extract*

Beat the egg whites with the cream of tartar into a soft meringue. White beating, gradually add ²/₃ of the sugar and the vanilla. Continue to beat until the meringue holds soft peaks. Combine the remaining sugar with the almonds, and carefully fold into the meringue. Line three large baking sheets, 15x16 inches (38x40 cm), with non-stick baking paper and spread ¹/₃ of the meringue on each. If you have a convection oven, bake all three together at 300°F (175°C) for 30-40 minutes. Otherwise, bake them separately. Cool and remove paper. Combine chocolate and corn oil in a double boiler and stir until melted. Brush one side of the meringues with the melted chocolate. Refrigerate until set. Turn over, brush the other sides with remaining chocolate, and chill again until firm. Cut the meringues lengthwise in half with a sharp knife. Whip the cream with the sugar and the vanilla, until light and fluffy. Place the meringue layers on top of each other, spreading the whipped cream in between. Garnish with whipped cream rosettes and fresh raspberries or chocolate-covered almonds. Refrigerate uncovered.

Preparation time 3-4 hours

Wedding Cake

The wedding cake is the sweet finale of the most important day of our lives. It is the culmination of the dream the young couple lives on their wedding day. You can prepare it at home with simple ingredients found in the supermarket. Fill it with strawberries, dress it in white and garnish it with pink roses and green leaves. Its spectacular appearance, as well as its taste, will captivate everyone present.

1	wedding cake stand with three bases
3	round cake pans with diameters 6 in (15 cm), 9 in (23 cm) and 12 in (30 cm)
5	dozen small pink candy roses with green leaves
5	yards (meters) pleated organza netting

The Cake

10	large eggs
2½	cups self-rising cake flour
2	teaspoons vanilla extract
2½	cups sugar
1/2	cup cooled melted unsalted butter

Leave the eggs at room temperature for several hours. Sift the flour. Beat 5 eggs and half the sugar with an electric mixer at high speed, until thick and fluffy, about 15 minutes. Gradually sift half the flour, on top of the eggs, and gently, fold in. Carefully stir in half the butter and mix well. Pour batter into the large cake pan, lined with non-stick baking paper. Prepare batter with the remaining ingredients in the same manner and divide between the medium and small cake pans. If you have a convection oven, you can bake three cakes together at 350°F (180°C) for about 35 minutes. Otherwise, bake them separately. Cool and freeze until ready to use.

Butter Cream Filling

1¾	cups sugar
5	egg whites
1/2	teaspoon cream of tartar
2/3	cup unsalted butter, softened
1	teaspoon vanilla extract

Put the sugar in a saucepan with ½ cup of water. Bring the mixture to a boil over medium heat, and cook or simmer until the syrup reaches to the soft ball stage, 240°F (116°C) on a candy thermometer. Remove the saucepan from the heat and set in a bowl of cold water, to stabilize the temperature. Beat the egg whites with the cream of tartar at high speed, to a soft peak meringue. With the mixer on, add the slightly cooled syrup in a thin steady stream and con-

tinue beating for another 5 minutes until the meringue is stiff and glossy. Cool completely. Beat the butter and vanilla with the mixer until light and fluffy. Beating at low speed, gradually add the meringue, taking care not to deflate. Cover with plastic wrap and refrigerate. Bring to room temperature before using. You can substitute the butter cream filling with the following whipped cream filling:

4	teaspoons unflavored gelatin
1/4	cup cold water
4	cups whipping cream
1	cup powdered sugar
1	teaspoon vanilla extract

Sprinkle the gelatin on the water and dissolve over low heat. Cool slightly. Whip the cream with the sugar and vanilla until slightly thickened. Continue beating on low speed, while gradually adding the dissolved gelatin. Increase speed to high and beat until stiff. Refrigerate until ready to use. Cover the wedding cake with pliable rolled fondant which is available commercially as "Regalice", or you can make your own with:

2	tablespoons powdered gelatin
1/2	cup cold water
1	cup corn syrup
2	tablespoon glycerine
4	tablespoons vegetable shortening
1/4	teaspoons almond extract
4½	lbs (2 kg) powdered sugar

Sprinkle the gelatin on the water and dissolve over low heat or in a double boiler. Add the corn syrup and glycerine and mix well. Stir in the shortening and before it completely melts, remove from the heat and add the almond extract. Cool slightly. Put half the sugar in a bowl and make a well in the center. Pour in the gelatin mixture and with a wooden spoon gradually incorporate the sugar from the sides of the bowl, until the mixture is no longer sticky. Gradually add the remaining sugar and knead until smooth and pliable. If it is too soft, add more powdered sugar. Use the fondant immediately or wrap airtight and refrigerate until ready to use. To use, allow it to reach room temperature and knead until it softens.

Assemble the Wedding Cake: Slice the cakes in half horizontally and fill with the butter or whipped cream and strawberries. Spread the top and sides of the cakes with a little butter cream frosting. Dust the work surface with powdered sugar, sifted with a little cornstarch, and roll out a thin sheet of fondant large enough to completely cover the top surface and sides of the first cake. Evenly trim the edge around the base of the cake. Repeat the same procedure for the other two cakes. To make the garland ruffles, roll out more fondant and cut round "collars"; with the handle of a wooden spoon dipped in cornstarch, make indentations around the edge. Affix the garlands around the sides of the cake and arrange the candy roses on top brushing with a little butter cream, so they will stay in place. On the top most cake, place two plastic champagne glasses joined with a pink satin ribbon.

Preparation time depends entirely on your patience and ability,

BABY'S CHRISTENING

MENU

Mincemeat Pâté or
Fried Canapés

Shrimp in Aspic

Fillets with Avocado Béarnaise or
Fillet of Veal Taurnedos
Potatoes Anna or Spinach Soufflé

Salad Served in Glasses

Orange Bavarian Cream or
Pineapple Dessert
Ice Cream Swans

Sparkling White Wine and Ruby Cabernet

Mincemeat Pâté

20   strips of bacon
1   lb (500 gr) chicken livers
3   oz (90 gr) butter
2   large onions, grated
5   oz (125 gr) mushrooms, finely chopped
1   lb (400 gr) ground beef
6   oz (150 gr) ground pork
7   oz (200 gr) cooked ham, finely chopped
3   eggs
1/2   cup cream
*   salt and pepper, to taste*
1   tablespoon green peppercorns
1/4   teaspoon thyme
1/4   teaspoon minced bay leaves
2   tablespoons brandy
3   tablespoons sherry
*   radishes and a few bay leaves for garnish*

Butter a 6-cup ovenproof loaf pan. Cut the fat off the bacon strips with a scissors. Cover the bottom and sides of the pan with the fat. Set aside as many fat strips as needed to cover the top of the pâté. Finely chop the remaining bacon. Place the livers in cold salted water, and let stand 30 minutes. Drain and rinse well. Devein and skin the livers and chop them finely. Heat the butter in a saucepan and saute the onions, mushrooms, and bacon. Combine the onion mixture, livers, the ground meat, ham, eggs, cream,

brandy, sherry, and the spices in a bowl, kneading well with your hands. Empty into loaf pan, and cover the surface of the pâté with the reserved fat strips. Cover with aluminum foil. Place in a large baking pan, filled with warm water up to half the height of the loaf pan. Bake the pâté in a 350°F (180°C) oven for 1 hour and 30 minutes. Remove from oven and let it cool. Spread ample melted butter over the surface. Refrigerate for at least 48 hours, to develop flavor. The butter will harden, keeping the pâté fresh for up to two weeks. To serve, turn out onto a platter. Garnish with radishes and bay leaves.

Preparation time 2 hours

Fried Canapés

1   loaf of sliced bread
6   slices cooked ham
10   slices Swiss cheese, Gouda, kasseri or Cheddar
2   eggs, beaten with 1 tablespoon olive oil and a pinch of salt
*   fine bread crumbs*

Using a round 1 2/3 inch (4 cm) cookie cutter, cut round canapés out of the bread slices. Use a slightly smaller cookie cutter to cut rounds out of the cheese and ham slices. Assemble the canapés, layering one slice of cheese and one slice of ham between two slices of bread. Seal tightly in plastic bags and refrigerate or freeze, until served.

To cook, let them thaw first. Then roll each canapé separately in the beaten eggs, coating all sides, and dredge in bread crumbs. Fry in hot oil for about 1 minute on each side, until golden brown. Serve warm.

Preparation time 30 minutes

Shrimp in Aspic

3   lbs (1½ kg) fresh or frozen shrimp
1   cup white wine
2   cups water
1   bay leaf
2   tablespoons lemon juice
1/2 cup water
3   tablespoons unflavored gelatin
2   egg whites
3   8-oz packets (600 gr total) cream cheese
1   cup whipping cream
3/4 cup mayonnaise
1/2 cup finely chopped fresh dill
1   teaspoon Worcestershire sauce
2   garlic cloves, finely minced
1/4 teaspoon Tabasco sauce
2   tablespoons lemon juice
1/2 cup finely chopped pickled cucumbers
1/4 teaspoon herbs of Provence
     salt and freshly ground pepper
1/4 cup ketchup (optional)

Peel and devein the shrimp. Bring the water to a boil, with the wine, lemon juice, and bay leaf. Add the shrimp and cook for 5 minutes. Remove the shrimp and bay leaf with a slotted spoon. Discard the bay leaf and set aside the remaining shrimp stock. Stir the gelatin into 1/2 cup cold water and let swell. Add to the shrimp stock. Beat the egg whites until foamy and stir into the gelatin-shrimp stock. Stirring continuously, heat the mixture over high heat, just to the boiling point. Remove from heat and cool for 10 minutes. Reheat to the boiling point, and cool again for 10 minutes. Strain through a fine sieve lined with absorbent paper. This will clear the aspic mixture and make it transparent. Grease a wide, shallow, clam shell-shaped mold with corn oil. Pour half the aspic into the mold and refrigerate for 30 minutes, until slightly thickened. Arrange as many shrimp as will fit onto the aspic, with small sprigs of dill in between, and refrigerate. Chop the remaining shrimp finely and set aside. Beat the cream cheese in a large bowl, until it softens. Gradually add the cream and mayonnaise, a little at a time, stirring until smooth and uniform. Add the rest of the ingredients, the remaining aspic, and the chopped shrimp; stir well. Add ketchup, if desired. Carefully pour the mixture into the mold over the shrimp. Refrigerate overnight to set. To serve, dip the mold in warm water, cover with a platter and turn over, shaking lightly until the aspic falls onto the platter. Garnish with cucumber crescents and purslane sprigs or any other green leaves.

Preparation time 1 hour

Spinach Soufflé

3	tablespoons butter
1/3	cup finely chopped onion
1	lb (500 gr) frozen spinach, thawed and finely chopped
1/8	teaspoon nutmeg
1/3	cup grated cheese (Romano or Parmesan)
	salt and pepper, to taste
1/3	cup butter
3	tablespoons all-purpose flour
1¼	cups hot milk
5	egg yolks
7	egg whites
1/4	cup fine bread crumbs

Melt the 3 tablespoons butter in a saucepan and saute the onions until transparent. Place the spinach in a pan over low heat and stir, until it dries. Add the onions, nutmeg, cheese, salt and pepper, stir briefly and remove from heat. Melt the ¹/₃ cup butter in a saucepan, add the flour, and saute for 1 minute. Pour in the hot milk, stirring vigorously and cook until the sauce is smooth and thick. Cool slightly,

stir in the egg yolks one at a time, then mix in the spinach. At this stage, you may cover it and refrigerate. One hour before serving, beat the egg whites to a soft meringue. Fold into the soufflé mixture, taking care not to deflate the meringue. Butter a deep 7-cup ovenproof soufflé dish. Sprinkle with bread crumbs, shaking out excess. Empty the spinach mixture into the dish. Sprinkle the surface lightly with bread crumbs. Bake the soufflé in a 350°F (180°C) oven for 40-45 minutes. Serve immediately.

Preparation time 1 hour

Potatoes Anna

4¹/₂	lbs (2 kg) large potatoes
1	cup butter or margarine, clarified
	salt and pepper, to taste
1	cup grated mild kefalotiri cheese
1	cup whipping cream

To clarify the butter or margarine, melt in a small saucepan and skim the foam from the surface. Empty carefully into another container to cool, and discard the milky residue remaining at the bottom of the saucepan. Slice the potatoes as thinly as possible, as though for thick potato chips. For best results use the thick-slice setting of a food processor. Wipe the potato slices with paper towels. Heat $1/2$ cup clarified butter in a large pan over medium heat. Sauté the potatoes in 2 or 3 batches for 2-3 minutes, stirring and separating the slices with a spatula. Remove from heat and cool until they can be safely handled. Melt the remaining clarified butter in a round 8-inch (20-cm) teflon or aluminum baking pan. Starting at the center, arrange the potato slices in a spiral, overlapping one another, until the bottom is completely covered. Then cover the sides with overlapping potato slices. For proper support, the side slices must rest on the bottom layer. Fill the dish with more overlapping layers of potatoes, starting each one at the center, and sprinkling salt, pepper, kefalotiri cheese, and cream over each layer. Place a small dish on the surface and lightly press down on the potatoes. Place the pan in the middle of the oven on a wire rack, and place a larger pan below to catch any butter which may leak out. Bake in a very hot 465°F (240°C) oven for 20 minutes. Press the potatoes down again with the dish, and bake for an additional 40-50 minutes until golden brown. After removing from the oven, press again with the dish to remove excess butter. Turn the potatoes out onto an ovenproof dish and brown briefly under the broiler before serving.

Preparation time 2 hours

Alternatively, you can grate the potatoes using the thick grater setting of a food processor. Press between layers of absorbent paper to dry, and fry in hot oil. You may fry the potatoes well in advance. Served warm or cold, they are just as delicious.

Fillets with Avocado Béarnaise

8   fillets of beef
1/2   cup clarified butter
4   tablespoons brandy
       salt and pepper, to taste

       The Sauce
4   tablespoons white vinegar
1/2   cup white wine
2   fresh green onions, finely chopped
1/2   teaspoon tarragon
6   peppercorns, crushed
       salt and pepper, to taste
4   egg yolks
1/2   lb (250 gr) pats of cold butter
2   tablespoons lemon juice
1   ripe avocado
       finely chopped parsley

Flatten the fillets slightly with a wooden mallet. Melt half the clarified butter in a heavy skillet, over high heat, and saute 4 of the fillets until browned on all sides. Pour in half the brandy and shake the skillet over the heat until the brandy evaporates. Remove the fillets to a metal plate and keep warm. Add the rest of the clarified butter to the skillet and saute the remaining fillets in the same manner, quenching them with the rest of the brandy. Remove these to the metal plate. Mix the salt and pepper and sprinkle on the fillets. Serve the fillets with avocado béarnaise sauce.

Avocado béarnaise sauce: Boil the vinegar, wine, onions, tarragon, and peppercorns in a saucepan. Lower the temperature and simmer uncovered, until the liquid is reduced to $1/4$ of its original volume. Strain through a fine sieve, and cool to room temperature. Slightly beat the egg yolks in a bowl. Stir in the reduced liquid and transfer to a double boiler. Stir continuously until the sauce starts to thicken. Gradually add the pats of butter a few at a time, stirring continuously until blended and the sauce is thick and creamy. Remove from heat, add salt and pepper. Peel the avocado and puree in a food processor with the lemon juice for 1-2 minutes. Pour in the sauce and blend until smooth and uniform.

Preparation time 30 minutes

Fillet of Veal Tournedos

8   sliced veal fillets
4   oz (100 gr) clarified butter
8   thin slices foie gras

       The Sauce
2   tablespoons butter
2   tablespoons flour
2   tablespoons sugar
2   cups beef stock
1/3   cup Madeira or demi sec wine
1   tablespoon tomato paste
2-3   small white or black canned truffles, sliced
1   tablespoon of the truffle liquid (optional)
       salt and pepper

First prepare the Madeira sauce. Melt the butter in a medium-sized saucepan. Add the flour and cook, stirring over low heat for 2 minutes. Pour in the beef stock, half the wine, and the tomato paste, stirring vigorously until smooth. Simmer for about 30 minutes, until reduced to half its volume. In the meantime, stir 2 tablespoons sugar and 1 tablespoon water in a small saucepan and boil, until caramelized. Continue cooking until nearly black. Remove from heat and carefully add 2 tablespoons water; allow the caramel to cool. This process causes the sugar to lose its sweetness, and the resulting mixture is used to color various sauces. Add the caramel mixture with the rest of the ingredients to the reduced sauce, and simmer for 2 minutes. Add salt and pepper. Melt the butter in a frying pan and saute the fillets for 4 minutes on each side, for medium-rare. Saute the foie gras in the same frying pan, about 1 minute on each side. Place a slice on top of each fillet, and arrange them on a metal platter. Keep warm. Pour the sauce into the frying pan and stir, scraping up the residue. Bring just to the boiling point, and spoon the sauce over the fillets. Serve immediately.

Preparation time 40 minutes

Salad Served in Glasses

16 tender lettuce leaves (hearts)
3 tart red apples, cubed
3 green peppers, julienned
2 celery stalks, sliced
4 hard-boiled eggs, sliced crosswise
4 tablespoons finely chopped parsley
8 parsley sprigs

The Dressing
1/2 cup mayonnaise
1/4 cup whipping cream
1/4 cup white wine
     salt and pepper, to taste

Wash and drain the lettuce leaves. To shorten the leaves, cut off the bottom part of the stalks and chop. Mix the chopped lettuce with the apples, peppers, and celery in a bowl. Place 2 whole lettuce leaves upright in each of 8 ice cream glasses. Divide the salad evenly into the glasses. Arrange 2 slices of egg and a parsley sprig in each glass. Cover with plastic wrap and refrigerate. When ready to serve, combine the dressing ingredients in a bowl and mix until uniform. To serve, pour 2 teaspoons of dressing onto each salad. Sprinkle with finely chopped parsley.

Preparation time 20 minutes

Wholewheat Dinner Rolls

1   tablespoon dry yeast
4   cups wholewheat flour
1/2 cup cornmeal
1   cup bread flour
2   teaspoons salt
3   tablespoons corn oil
2   tablespoons molasses or brown sugar
1   cup lukewarm water 100°F (40°C)
1   cup lukewarm strong coffee 100°F (40°C)

Combine the yeast with the three flours in a small basin and mix thoroughly. Make a well in the center and pour in the salt, corn oil, molasses, water and coffee. Mix, gradually combining the flour from the sides, to form a pliable dough. Knead until the dough is smooth and no longer sticky. Let it rest for 10 minutes. Transfer to a floured work surface and knead, adding more flour if necessary, until smooth and elastic. Place in a lightly greased bowl. Cover and let rise in a warm humid place for about 1 hour and 30 minutes, until doubled in bulk. Punch the dough down, knead vigorously, and let rise again. Divide and roll out into 2 loaves, or 16 small rolls. Arrange the rolls on a floured baking sheet. Cover with a cloth and let rise in a warm humid place, until doubled in bulk. Sprinkle with flour and score the surface with a sharp knife. Bake the rolls in a 350°F (180°C) oven for 30-35 minutes until golden brown. Cool on a rack and seal in airtight bags before freezing.

Preparation time 2 hours and 30 minutes

Ice Cream Swans

4   egg whites
1/4 teaspoon cream of tartar
1   cup fine sugar
1   teaspoon vanilla extract
2   lbs (1 kg) vanilla ice cream
2   cups whipped cream

The Garnish
maraschino cherries or small strawberries

In a mixing bowl beat the egg whites with the cream of tartar at high speed, until thick and foamy. While beating at high speed, gradually add half the sugar, a little at a time, and continue beating, until the meringue holds soft peaks. Add the rest of the sugar, mixed with the vanilla, in two parts, blending at low speed, until all of it is incorporated into the meringue. The sugar added in this manner, makes the meringue light and airy when baked. Draw oval shapes on baking paper. Fill a pastry bag with meringue and pipe it on the ovals to form swan wings. Draw large "S"s on another sheet of baking paper and form the swan necks, piping the meringue through a plain 1/2 inch wide tip. Place the baking sheets on wire racks and bake in a 150°F (80°C) oven, with the fan on (if yours is a convection type) for about two hours. Turn the oven off and let the meringues cool inside with the door slightly ajar. Store them in a dry place, in an airtight tin. They will keep for up to six months. To assemble the swans, arrange large single scoops of ice cream on dessert plates. Using whipped cream, stick the wings on the left and right sides of the scoops. Pipe a garland of whipped cream on top of the ice cream, between the wings. Press the swan's neck into place, and garnish with a cherry or strawberry placed on the swan's back.

Preparation time 2 hours
and 30 minutes

Orange Bavarian Cream

2	oranges
7	egg yolks
1	cup sugar
2	teaspoons cornstarch
1½	cups warm milk
6	teaspoons unflavored gelatin
5	egg whites
1/2	cup heavy cream, whipped
3	tablespoons Grand Marnier

Lightly butter an 8-cup mold. Grate the zest off the unpeeled oranges. Cut the oranges and squeeze out their juice. Beat the egg yolks with the orange zest in a bowl, until the mixture is thick and foamy. While beating at medium speed, gradually add half the sugar, a little at a time, then the cornstarch and milk. Transfer the mixture to a heavy saucepan. Stir the gelatin into the orange juice and let swell. Add to the pan. Stirring continuously, cook over low heat until the custard is thick enough to cover the spoon. Cool slightly and stir in the liqueur. Set aside. Beat the egg whites to a soft meringue. While beating, add the remaining sugar, a little at a time. Fold the whipped cream

into the custard, then carefully fold in the meringue, taking care not to deflate the mixture. Empty into the prepared mold, and refrigerate for 24 hours. If using the butterfly mold shown in the picture, first prepare a bit of red and a bit of green gelatin and fill the small depressions with a syringe. Refrigerate to set, then fill with the Bavarian mixture. When ready to serve, dip the mold briefly into lukewarm water, cover it with a platter, and turn it over, shaking lightly, until the Bavarian falls out onto the plate. Refrigerate 1-2 hours before serving. For the antennas, use 2 green tendrils.

Preparation time 1 hour (refrigeration time is not included)

Pineapple Dessert

1	can pineapple 1 lb 12 oz (800 gr)
2	teaspoons unflavored gelatin
2	cups orange juice
2	tablespoons lemon juice
1/3	cup sugar
2	egg yolks, lightly beaten

The Garnish
caramelized orange peel
| 3 | pineapple slices |

maraschino cherries

Puree all but 3 slices of the pineapple in a food processor, until smooth. Stir the gelatin in $1/2$ cup orange juice and let swell. Place the gelatin in a double boiler. Add the sugar and egg yolks. Beat until the gelatin and the sugar dissolve. Add the remaining orange and lemon juice. Stir for 1-2 minutes over the simmering water, remove from heat and pour into the food processor containing the pineapple. Process a few seconds. Empty into an 8-cup ring mold and refrigerate, until set. For best results, refrigerate overnight. Unmold onto a platter and garnish with halved pineapple slices, cherries, and caramelized orange peel, prepared according to the recipe, "Caramelized Oranges" (page 70). Refrigerate dessert until ready to serve.

Preparation time 30 minute

Organizing your Baby's Christening

Give your child's godparents a real treat with this fine, eclectic menu. If the christening is in summer, and you are planning to set the table in the garden or on the veranda, do be prepared

in case the weather is not accommodating. Garden tables should be set only shortly before serving the meal. Be sure to have the tableware and linens ready for either case. Serve sparkling white wine with the appetizers and the first course, and dry red wine with the fillets.

❧ *Each recipe serves 8-10 persons.*
❧ *Well in advance, prepare the canapés and the rolls. Store them in the freezer. Also prepare the meringue for the swans and store in airtight tins.*
❧ *Three days in advance, prepare the pâté and store in the refrigerator.*
❧ *Two days in advance, prepare the Bavarian or the pineapple dessert. Prepare the potatoes Anna, place in the baking pan and refrigerate.*
❧ *The day before, prepare the shrimp in aspic and make the spinach soufflé up to the stage the egg whites are to be added. Wash and chop the vegetables for the salad, except for the apples, and boil the eggs.*
❧ *In the morning, put together the ice cream swans and store in the freezer. Take the canapés and the rolls out of the freezer. Cut the apples and place the salad in the glasses. Prepare the Madeira sauce.*
❧ *Shortly before serving, fry the canapés and prepare the fillets.*

MOONLIGHT BARBECUE

MENU

Stuffed Clams

❧

Charcoal Broiled Seafood
Lobster Cardinal

❧

Summer Salad

❧

Onion Bread (Focaccia)

❧

Cheese Platter

❧

Fruit Platter
Ice Cream Puffs or Brandy Snaps

❧

Light Bouquet Chenin Blanc

Stuffed Clams

36   clams
1/2   cup butter
4   oz (100 gr) spinach, blanched and drained
3   tablespoons finely chopped parsley
3   tablespoons finely chopped celery
3   tablespoons finely chopped green onion
3   tablespoons fine bread crumbs
15   drops Tabasco sauce
      salt and pepper, to taste

Seafood should never be cooked too long, because the meat toughens. The easiest way to open clams, is to boil them in a minimal amount of water over high heat with fresh herbs so that they acquire flavor. As soon as they open, remove from the pot. Another method, better when the clam meat should be cooked, combined with other ingredients, is to refrigerate them covered for a few hours. When they open halfway, simply stick the point of a knife into the gap and separate the shells. Discard any clams that don't open. Remove the clam meat. Cut away and discard the little sand-filled sacks. Set aside a small piece from each clam for garnish. Use scissors to finely cut the rest of the meat. Heat the butter in a saucepan, stir in the spinach, parsley, celery, onion, bread crumbs, and Tabasco over low heat for 15 minutes. Remove from heat, and press the mixture through a food mill, or process for a few seconds in a blender. Mix with the clam meat in a bowl. Fill each shell with about 1 teaspoon of the mixture and garnish with the reserved pieces of clam. Bake the shells in a 425°F (220°C) oven for 10 minutes. Transfer to a platter and serve immediately.

Preparation time 40 minutes

Charcoal-Broiled Seafood

2   lbs (1 kg) mussels in the shell
2   small frozen octopus
2   lbs (1 kg) large shrimp, peeled and deveined (heads and tail intact)

Garlic Sauce
6   garlic cloves, mashed
2   egg yolks
1   cup fresh basil leaves

1   cup olive oil
2   tablespoons lemon juice

Oriental Sauce
1/2   cup soy sauce
1/2   cup oyster sauce
2   teaspoons sugar
2   teaspoons cornstarch
1   tablespoon lemon juice
1/4   teaspoon ground ginger

Lemon Tartar Sauce
1   tablespoon fine capers, mashed
2   tablespoons finely chopped pickles
1   tablespoon finely chopped green onion
1/2   teaspoon finely chopped mint leaves
1   cup mayonnaise
1   tablespoon lemon juice
      freshly ground pepper

Brush the octopus and shrimp with olive oil, cover and refrigerate. Scrub the mussels with a hard brush under running water, and remove the beards. Prepare at least two of the three recommended sauces, for these are what will give the seafood its special taste.

Garlic sauce: Process the garlic with the egg yolks in a blender, until smooth. Add the basil and 1/3 of the oil, blend until smooth. Continue processing while adding the rest of the oil in a thin, steady stream, until the mixture thickens. Add as much lemon juice, as desired.

Oriental Sauce: Heat the ingredients in a saucepan. Simmer until mixture is clear and light.

Lemon Tartar Sauce: Combine the ingredients in a bowl, stir well. Add as much pepper as desired.

Broil the seafood shortly before serving. Arrange the shrimp in an oiled double wire rack and close it, fixing them in place. Do the same with the octopus, spreading them open as wide as possible between the two wire racks. Arrange the mussels side by side in a wide baking pan, sprinkle with a small amount of white wine, and cover. Place the wire racks with the seafood 4 inches over the fire, and broil the shrimp and the octopus briefly on both sides, taking care not to dry them out (about 2-3 minutes per side for the shrimp, 8-10 minutes per side for the octopus). Place the pan with the mussels on the rack over the charcoal. Broil for 5-7 minutes, until the shells open. Arrange the seafood on a platter and serve immediately accompanied by the sauces.

Preparation time 4 hours

Lobster Cardinal

1	large lobster 3-4 lbs (1½-2 kg)
1	carrot
1	small onion
1	celery stalk
	salt and peppercorns
1½	cups milk
3	tablespoons butter
3	tablespoons flour
1/2	cup fish stock
2-3	tablespoons juice from canned truffles
3	tablespoons cream
2-3	pats butter
1/8	teaspoon cayenne pepper

Fill a large pot with ample water. Add the carrot, onion, celery, ample salt, and 20 cracked peppercorns. Cover and boil for 10 minutes. Lower the live lobster carefully into the boiling water (head first, as this will kill it instantly), and boil for 6 minutes. Pour out most of the water leaving 2-3 cups and simmer for 15 minutes. If the lobster is too big for the pot, after immersing it in boiling water, place in a deep ovenproof pan, pour ample hot water over it, cover with aluminum foil and bake in a 350°F (180°C) oven for 30 minutes. Drain and allow to cool. Cut and separate the head from the body. Carefully remove the meat from head and claws with a special utensil, taking care not to break them. Slit open the abdomen and remove the tail meat. Slice it crosswise and discard the black vein. **Prepare the Cardinal sauce:** Saute the flour in butter for 1 minute. Add the milk, stirring vigorously and simmer until the sauce thickens. Add the fish stock and the truffle juice. Simmer until the sauce is reduced to about 3/4 of its original volume. Remove from heat and stir in the cream, butter, and cayenne pepper. Assemble the head and tail shell of lobster on a platter. Place the pieces of meat from the head and claws inside the shell and pour a small amount of sauce over it. Arrange the sliced tail pieces on top. Pour some hot sauce over it and spinkle with the finely chopped parsley. Serve the rest of the sauce hot in a gravy boat. Serve the dish hot.

Preparation time 1 hour and 30 minutes

Saffron-Mayonnaise Sauce

2	tablespoons brandy
	pinch of finely chopped garlic
1	cup mayonnaise
1	teaspoon prepared mustard
1	pinch saffron powder
1/4	cup sour cream

1   tablespoon mashed capers
1   tablespoon finely chopped green onion

Simmer the brandy with the garlic in a small saucepan until 1 tablespoon remains. Allow to cool and combine with the mayonnaise, mustard, saffron, and sour cream in a food processor. Blend for 30 seconds, until smooth and uniform. Add the mashed capers and green onion and process an additional 30 seconds. Cooked lobster can be served cold accompanied by this tangy sauce instead of cardinal sauce. The dish is convenient to prepare in advance and refrigerate until served.

Cheese Platter

Arrange various cheeses on an attractive wooden tray, and decorate with rings cut from red and green peppers. Also garnish with fruits. Fruits, especially grapes, not only look beautiful, they also complement the flavor of nearly all cheeses.

Summer Salad

2   large tomatoes
1   large cucumber
1   green bell pepper
1   red bell pepper
1   small onion
    The Dressing
1/3 cup olive oil
2   tablespoons vinegar
1   tablespoon finely chopped fresh basil
1   tablespoon finely chopped parsley
    salt and pepper, to taste
1/2 teaspoon oregano

Wash and clean the vegetables. Cut into small cubes and mix together in a salad bowl. Cover with plastic wrap and refrigerate. To serve the salad, combine the dressing ingre--dients in a jar and shake vigorously. Pour the dressing over the salad just before serving.   Preparation time 30 minutes

Onion Bread (Focaccia)

5¹/₂ cups all-purpose flour
2   tablespoons dry yeast
2   cups lukewarm water 100°F (40°C)
1   tablespoon sugar
1/4 cup olive oil
2   teaspoons salt

    The Garnish
1/4 cup olive oil
2   large onions, sliced
1   garlic clove, crushed
2   tablespoons finely chopped fresh basil
1/2 teaspoon oregano
    salt and pepper, to taste

Combine the yeast with the flour in a large bowl. Make a well in the center and pour in the rest of the ingredients. Gradually taking the flour from the sides, mix until the dough is soft and no longer sticky. Add flour as needed and knead until smooth and elastic. Cover the dough and let rise in a warm humid place, until doubled in bulk. Meanwhile, saute the onions and garlic in hot oil, until transparent. Remove from heat. Punch the dough down and knead for 5 minutes. Spread into a greased 16-inch (40-cm) baking pan. Cover and let rise. Brush the surface with a small amount of olive oil. Using two fingers, make deep impressions in the dough all over the surface. Spread the sauteed onions on top and sprinkle with basil, oregano, salt, and pepper. Bake in a 400°F (200°C) oven for about 45 minutes until golden brown. Remove from oven and cut the bread into squares. Serve while still slightly warm, or reheat before serving.

Preparation time 2 hours and 30 minutes

Preparation time 30 minutes

Brandy Snaps

1/3   cup butter
1/2   cup light brown sugar
1/3   cup molasses or light corn syrup
1/4   teaspoon ground ginger
1/4   teaspoon cinammon (optional)
1   teaspoon orange zest
1/3   cup all-purpose flour
2   tablespoons brandy
2   cups whipped cream
       strawberries or raspberries

Combine the first six ingredients in a small saucepan over low heat. Stir until the butter melts and starts to sizzle. Remove from heat. Add the flour and the brandy and stir until smooth and uniform. Cool to room temperature. Line a baking sheet with non-stick baking paper. Drop well-spaced tablespoons of the batter on the sheet, forming them into small circles. Remember that they will spread out while baking. Make only three at a time as they harden very quickly when removed from the oven, and are difficult to shape. Bake the snaps in a 340°F (175°C) oven for 10 to 12 minutes, until golden brown. Remove from oven, let cool for 1 minute. Lift them one by one with the edge of a small spatula and immediately wrap them around the handle of a

Ice Cream Puffs

25   cream puff shells
2   lbs (1 kg) vanilla ice cream
4   oz (125 gr) semi-sweet baking chocolate or chips
1/3 cup whipping cream

You may use commercially-made cream puff shells or make them at home. Boil 1 cup water with 1/2 cup butter and a pinch of salt. Add 1 cup flour and stir vigorously with a wooden spoon until the dough gathers around the spoon in a ball. Transfer to a mixing bowl. While beating the dough with a dough hook, add 4 eggs one by one and continue beating until eggs are smoothly incorporated into the dough. Transfer to a pastry bag fitted with a plain tip and pipe small rosettes on a baking sheet. Bake in a 425°F (220°C) oven for 15 minutes, then continue baking at 300°F (150°C) for an additional 25 minutes, until dry. Remove from oven, allow to cool and seal in plastic bags, before freezing. On the day before serving, slash each puff in the middle and fill with ice cream. Store in freezer.

Prepare the chocolate sauce: Place the chocolate and cream in a saucepan and stir over low heat until smooth. Cool briefly before using. To prepare the chocolate vine leaves, thoroughly wash a few vine leaves with the stems and wipe with absorbent paper. Then follow the procedure as for the Chocolate Tarts (page 97). When ready to serve, arrange the ice cream puffs on a platter to resemble a bunch of grapes. Pour the chocolate sauce over them. Place the chocolate vine leaves at the top. Serve im-

thick wooden spoon, creating little rolls. Or wrap them around metal cones. Also you may place the brandy snaps into small, 4-inch (10-cm) metal bowls and flute the edges, to make cup shapes. If the brandy snaps harden before you remove them from the baking pan, place them in the oven again for several seconds. Continue baking and forming the brandy snaps until the mixture is used up. Keep in airtight containers, and store in a dry place. Also they can be frozen. To serve, fill with whipped cream. Serve them accompanied by strawberries or raspberries.

Preparation time 1-2 hours

Fruit Platter

Create your own beautiful design using various fresh fruits in season. You can make the one in the picture. Cut the melon into flat circular slices, each about $1/_2$ inch (1.5 cm) thick. Remove the seeds. Stack the slices at a slant and support with wooden skewers. Cut a small duck out of an apple and complete the platter by arranging the other fruits around the edge. The fruits shown here are melon, peach, apple, grapes, and maraschino cherries.

Organizing your Moonlight Barbecue

A warm night with a full moon in the heart of the summer is the perfect occasion to entertain. If you have a veranda or garden, invite a few good friends, or organize a large party for many guests. Grilled seafood is an easy and delicious meal that will satisfy your friends without overwhelming them. Serve a light bouquet white wine all the dinner through.

❀ *Each recipe serves 8 persons.*
❀ *Well in advance, prepare the cream puffs, brandy snaps, and bread. Store in the freezer.*
❀ *The day before, boil the live lobster as soon as you bring it home. Prepare the chocolate sauce and the saffron sauce; fill the puffs with ice cream and freeze.*
❀ *In the morning, prepare the clams and the seafood. Decorate the cheese platter. If you decide to serve lobster with saffron sauce, prepare and refrigerate.*
❀ *In the afternoon, mix the salad and prepare the fruit platter.*
❀ *30 minutes before serving, start the charcoal fire. Prepare the cardinal sauce.*
❀ *Shortly before serving, start grilling the clams and invite your friends to seat themselves.*
❀ *Once everyone is seated, serve the clams and start grilling the seafood.*

SILVER ANNIVERSARY

MENU
Salmon Sponge Appetizer or
Vol-au-Vents with Ham and Mushrooms

Seafood Crepes

Fillet Chateaubriand
Mushrooms à la Crème
Potatoes Duchesse

Multicolored Salad

Chocolate Mousse Cake
Strawberry Crepes

Sauvignon Blance and Ruby Cabernet, Wines

Organizing Your Silver Anniversary

Twenty-five years of marriage is a significant milestone in the life of any couple. A silver wedding anniversary calls for a glittering celebration. If you have decided not to hold a large formal gathering, commemorate the special occasion by inviting a few close friends and preparing this gourmet menu, (which can be easily adapted to serve a larger number of guests). Doubling the amounts specified in the recipes allows you to serve 18 people. Start with the spectacular tricolor salmon sponge appetizer, followed by the delicately flavored seafood crepes. Complete the menu with an elegant French course-Chateaubriand with potatoes duchesse and mushrooms à la crème. For the finale, serve crepes with whipped cream and strawberries, a sublime dessert that melts in your mouth. Or try the chocolate mousse cake, just as light and soft, a true taste sensation. Fold the napkins and stand them in the glasses. As a centerpiece arrange white chrysanthemums, pink zinnias, and yellow roses in a low, oval base. Accompany this special dinner with white wine for the first course, and a dry red wine for the main course.

❀ Each recipe serves 8 persons.

❀ Well in advance, prepare the salmon sponge appetizer or the vol-au-vents; also prepare the seafood crepes and the rolls. Freeze each of them at the stage specified in the recipes.

❀ The day before, prepare the chocolate mousse cake and cut the vegetables for the salad. Refrigerate. Prepare everything you need to cook the crepes.

❀ The evening before, set the table and make the preliminary preparations for the fillet.

❀ In the morning, remove pre-prepared foods from the freezer. Prepare the mushrooms à la crème and the potatoes duchesse, without baking them. Fill the crepes with strawberries. Refrigerate everything until ready to serve.

❀ In the afternoon, bake the fillet and prepare the sauce. Bake the crepes.

❀ While eating the crepes, bake the potatoes duchesse.

Salmon Sponge Appetizer

The Sponge Base
2½ tablespoons butter
1/3 cup flour
1¾ cup milk
2 teaspoons lemon juice
   salt and pepper, to taste
3 egg yolks
4 egg whites

The Pink Filling
4 oz (100 gr) finely chopped salmon
7 oz (200 gr) cream cheese
1 tablespoon lemon juice
1 teaspoon tomato paste

The Green Filling
7 oz (200 gr) cream cheese
3 tablespoons finely chopped green onion
3 tablespoons finely chopped dill
1/2 teaspoon lemon juice
   pinch of garlic (optional)
   salt and pepper, to taste

The White Topping
7 oz (200 gr) cream cheese
2 teaspoons ground green peppercorns
1/4 teaspoon lemon juice

2 tablespoons horseradish sauce

The Garnish
cone-shaped salmon slices
halved lemon slices
green pepper dewdrops

Heat the butter and the flour in a saucepan over medium heat; add the milk and stir vigorously for 1 minute until thick and smooth. Add the lemon juice, salt and pepper and remove from heat. Cool the sauce slightly, blend in the egg yolks and set aside. Beat the egg whites into a soft meringue and carefully fold into the sauce. Line a jelly roll pan with baking paper and lightly butter. Spread the batter evenly over the entire surface. Bake in a 350°F (180°C) oven for about 30 minutes, or until golden brown. Allow to cool and turn it over onto waxpaper. Carefully remove the baking paper and cut the sponge crosswise into three equal rectangular pieces. Blend the ingredients for each of the three fillings separately in a food processor, until smooth. Place one sponge piece on a platter. Spread the surface evenly with the pink filling. Place the second piece of sponge on top, and spread with the green filling. Set the third piece on top and spread with the white filling. At this stage, the appetizer can be frozen. To serve, thaw and garnish the top with salmon, halvedlemon slices and green pepper dewdrops.

Preparation time 1 hour and 30 minutes

Vol-au-Vents with Ham and Mushrooms

16   *miniature vol-au-vent pastry shells*
1   *tablespoon butter*
1   *tablespoon finely chopped green onion*
1   *cup finely sliced mushrooms*
1/2   *cup finely chopped ham*
1/4   *cup whipping cream*
1   *egg yolk*
1/2   *cup grated Romano or pecorino cheese*
    salt and pepper, to taste
1   *tablespoon finely chopped parsley*

Use ready-made miniature vol-au-vent pastry shells or make your own according to the recipe for Vol-au-Vent (Puff Pastries) (page 181) using 1½ inch (4 cm) round cookie cutters. Heat butter in a saucepan and saute the onion until transparent. Add mushrooms and ham, and stir over medium heat for 3-4 minutes. Remove from heat and cool slightly. Beat the cream with the egg yolk and fold into the mushroom mixture along with the cheeses. Add salt, freshly ground pepper, and parsley. Stir well, and fill the pastry shells. Allow to cool completely. Seal in airtight plastic bags and freeze until ready to serve. To serve, remove them from the freezer and immediately bake in a 400°F (200°C) oven for about 20 minutes, until golden brown. Serve warm.
Preparation time 35 minutes (using ready-made pastry shells)

Seafood Crepes

1   *lb (500 gr) fillet of sole*
1   *lb (500 gr) shrimp*
5   *oz (125 gr) crab legs*
1   *cup water*
1/2   *cup white wine*
1   *small onion, sliced*
1/4   *cup butter*
3   *tablespoons flour*
1/2   *cup whipping cream*
    salt and pepper, to taste
3   *green onions, finely chopped*
2   *tablespoons extra butter*
2   *tablespoons finely chopped parsley*
3   *tablespoons bread crumbs*
1/2   *cup grated Cheddar cheese*
10-12 *crepes*

Peel, devein, and rinse the shrimp. Reserve the shells. Put the water, wine, onion, and shrimp shells in a large pan and bring to a boil. Simmer about 20 minutes, until reduced to

about one cup. Strain the stock through a fine sieve and set aside. Heat the butter in a saucepan and saute the flour for 1 minute. Add the shrimp stock and stir over medium heat until the sauce is thick. Add the cream, salt and pepper and bring to a boil, stirring continuously. Remove from heat and set aside. Heat the butter in a separate saucepan and saute the onion. Add the shrimp, sole, and crab legs. Stir over high heat, until the liquid is absorbed. Combine the seafood with the sauce. Divide the seafood filling into 10-12 portions, and place in the center of each crepe. Fold the edges up encasing the filling. Arrange the stuffed crepes, folded side up, in an ovenproof dish. Combine the parsley, bread crumbs and cheese; sprinkle over the crepes. At this stage you may freeze or store them in the refrigerator until ready to serve. To serve, bake the crepes in a very hot oven until heated through. Alternatively, you can substitute lobster for the shrimp, or replace the sole with an equal amount of crab meat. Use a completely different combination of seafood, if desired.

Preparation time 1 hour and 30 minutes

Hollandaise Sauce with Asparagus

4   egg yolks
1   tablespoon lemon juice
5   oz (125 gr) clarified butter
9   oz (250 gr) asparagus, cooked and chopped

Process the egg yolks with the lemon juice in a food processor, until smooth and uniform. With the motor running, pour the hot butter, in a thin steady stream, through the opening. Add the asparagus and blend until the sauce is smooth and creamy.

Preparation time 15 minutes

Mushrooms à la Crème

2   tablespoons clarified butter
1   tablespoon minced onion
1   cup mushrooms
1/4 cup white wine
    salt and pepper, to taste
1   cup whipping cream
4   oz (100 gr) Roquefort or blue cheese (optional)
1   tablespoon finely chopped parsley

Heat the butter in a saucepan and saute the onion. Add the mushrooms (whole if small, sliced if large) and saute until wilted. Add the wine. Mash the cheese with a fork and stir in the cream, a little at a time. Pour the cheese sauce into the mushrooms and simmer, stirring, until thick. Add salt, freshly ground pepper, and parsley. Garnish the potato nests with a few mushrooms and serve the rest separately.

Preparation time 15 minutes

Fillet Chateaubriand

3	lbs (1½ kg) beef fillet
1	cup olive oil
	salt and pepper, to taste
3/4	cup white wine, combined with
1/4	cup brandy

The Sauce
1	cup Madeira wine
2	tablespoons flour
1	cup beef stock

Salt and pepper the meat and amply brush with olive oil. Refrigerate for several hours, occasionally turning over and brushing with more oil. Place the meat in a roasting pan and roast in a very hot 475°F (250°C) oven for 10 minutes. Open the oven and pour the wine and brandy mixture over the fillet, moistening the entire surface. Close the oven and lower the temperature to 400°F (200°C). Roast for an additional 10 minutes. Serve the fillet hot or cold, accompanied by potatoes duchesse, mushrooms à la crème, and various warm or cold sauces.

Madeira Sauce: Remove the roast fillet from the roasting pan. Empty the juices into a saucepan. Scrape the residue in the pan with the Madeira wine, or any demi-sec wine and pour into the juices. Skim the fat from the surface of the juices and transfer to another saucepan. Stir the flour into 2-3 tablespoons fat, over medium heat, until lightly brown. Stirring continuously, add the wine with the meat juices and continue cooking until slightly thickened. Add the beef stock or demi-glace sauce. Simmer, stirring at intervals, until the sauce is smooth and thick. Remove from the heat, adjust the seasoning and serve the sauce hot.

Preparation time 1 hour and 30 minutes

Potatoes Duchesse

2	cups stiff mashed potatoes
3	egg yolks
3	tablespoons butter
2	tablespoons whipping cream
	salt, pepper and nutmeg, to taste
1/2	cup grated mild kefalotiri or Parmesan cheese

Blend the egg yolks into the mashed potatoes one at a time, then fold in the butter, cream, and seasonings. Transfer to a pastry bag, fitted with a star-shaped tip. Pipe the mixture in round nest shapes, on a buttered and floured baking sheet or on buttered baking paper. Sprinkle the surfaces with the grated cheese, and refrigerate until ready to serve. Half an hour before serving, brown the potatoes duchesse in a 400°F (200°C) oven for about 15 minutes. Serve hot, filled with mushrooms à la crème and arranged around the fillet.

Preparation time 35 minutes

Multicolored Salad

1½	cups cooked peas
1	very small onion, sliced into thin rings
2	green onions, chopped
1	small tomato, sliced

3	small, tender zucchinis, chopped
2	slices cooked ham, chopped
1	small apple, sliced
1	small yellow bell pepper, chopped
1	cucumber, sliced into rounds
1	tablespoon finely chopped parsley
1	cup cooked corn
1	small red bell pepper, finely chopped
1	small green bell pepper, finely chopped
1	tablespoon finely chopped fresh dill
2	green onions, finely chopped
1	cup finely chopped red cabbage

Mix the first four ingredients in a salad bowl. In a second bowl, mix the next four ingredients. In a third bowl, mix the cucumber with the parsley. Mix the remaining ingredients, except for the red cabbage, in a fourth bowl. On a large round platter, arrange the five vegetable mixtures in circles with the red cabbage in the center, surrounded by the corn, then the cucumbers, yellow peppers and zucchini, and the pea mixture around the edge. Cover the salad with plastic wrap and refrigerate.

The Dressing
1	ripe avocado, mashed
2	tablespoons lemon juice
1	very small garlic clove, mashed
2	tablespoons finely chopped green onion
1	tablespoon finely chopped green bell pepper
1/2	cup olive oil
1	tablespoon vinegar
	salt and pepper, to taste

Blend the dressing ingredients in a food processor for 1-2 minutes, until smooth and creamy. Remove ¹/₃ of the dressing and fold in 1 tablespoon sour cream. Pour this over the zucchinis. Pour the rest of the dressing on the other vegetables. Prepare the dressing and dress the salad shortly before serving.

Preparation time 30 minutes

Strawberry Crepes

The Crepes
1   recipe crepes (page 23)

The Filling
1   lb (500 gr) strawberries
4   cups whipped cream
1   cup strawberry sauce

Prepare the crepes as in the recipe (page 23). Wash and drain the strawberries on paper towels. Reserve 6-7 perfect ones and set aside (stems intact). Slice half the strawberries. Put the rest in a sausepan with 1 cup water and simmer covered 5-6 minutes. Strain and discard the strawberries, reserving the liquid. If it is more than 1 cup, simmer until reduced to 1 cup. Add 2 tablespoons cornstarch, 3 tablespoons sugar, and 1 tablespoon lemon juice. Stir over low heat until the sauce is thick and clear. Remove from heat and allow to cool. Stir in 1 tablespoon brandy. Cover half of each crepe with 2 tablespoons whipped cream piped out of a pastry bag. Place a few strawberry slices on the whipped cream, and pour on 1 tablespoon strawberry sauce. Fold the crepes in half over the filling, then carefully fold them into quarters. Arrange the filled crepes in a circle around the outer edge of a round platter, slightly overlapping each other. Fill the center with whipped cream rosettes and arrange the reserved straw-

berries on top. Refrigerate several hours, before serving. When ready to serve, fill the piping bag with melted chocolate and pipe it through a fine tip over the crepes. If you wish to make banana crepes, slice 6 ripe bananas. Melt $1/3$ cup clarified butter with $1/3$ cup sugar, 2 tablespoons lemon juice, and 1 teaspoon lemon zest in a frying pan. Add the bananas and gently stir over medium heat until they are glazed. Cool to room temperature, sprinkle with a little cinnamon. Use this filling in place of strawberries.

Preparation time 1 hour

Chocolate Mousse Cake

The Sponge
3/4   cup cocoa
2   teaspoons baking powder
6   eggs, separated
1   cup sugar
1/2   teaspoon cream of tartar
1   teaspoon vanilla extract

The Filling
1/2   lb (250 gr) semi-sweet baking chocolate, or chips
4   eggs, separated
2   tablespoons brandy
2   tablespoons evaporated milk
2/3   cup sugar

The Garnish
white and dark chocolate curls

Beat the egg yolks with $\frac{1}{3}$ cup sugar and vanilla, until thick and creamy. In another bowl, beat the egg whites and cream of tartar, until foamy. While beating on high speed, gradually add the remaining sugar and continue beating, until the meringue holds soft peaks. Fold the cocoa and the meringue into the egg yolks, taking care not to deflate the meringue. Line two 10-inch (25-cm) cake pans with lightly buttered baking paper. Divide the batter between them and bake in a 350°F (180°C) oven for about 20 minutes, until they test done with a toothpick. Allow to cool, turn the sponges out, and carefully remove the baking paper.

The Filling: Melt the chocolate in a saucepan over low heat or preferably in a double boiler. Beat the egg yolks lightly with the brandy and milk. Fold into the chocolate, stirring continuously. Remove from the heat and cool to lukewarm. Meanwhile, beat the egg whites into a soft meringue. Gently fold the meringue into the chocolate, taking care not to deflate. Place sponge layers on a platter and spread some of the chocolate mousse in between. Frost the top and sides with the rest of the mousse. Using a vegetable peeler, cut curls from the dark and white chocolate, and let them fall randomly on the mousse until it is completely covered. Cover with plastic wrap and refrigerate, until ready to serve.

Preparation time 1 hour and 30 minutes

French Rolls

The Dough
4	cups bread flour
1	tablespoon dry yeast or
1	oz (30 gr) compressed yeast
2	tablespoons sugar
1	cup lukewarm milk 100°F (40°C)
2	tablespoons melted butter
1½	teaspoons salt
1½	teaspoons ground ginger

The Design Batter
1/2	cup flour
1/3	cup water

The Glaze
1	tablespoon sugar
1	teaspoon unflavored gelatin
1-2	tablespoons warm water

Combine the yeast with the flour, sugar, ginger, and salt. If using compressed yeast, dissolve it in milk and let rise until foamy. Put the dry ingredients in a large basin and make a well in the center. Pour in the milk, and melted butter. Mix together, gradually taking flour from the sides, until a sticky dough is formed. Turn onto a floured work surface and knead, adding more flour, if necessary, until the dough is soft and pliable and no longer sticky. Cover the dough and let rise in a warm humid place, until doubled in bulk. Punch the dough down. Form round rolls and place well apart on a greased baking sheet. Cover and let them rise until doubled in bulk.

The Design Batter: Mix $\frac{1}{2}$ cup flour with $\frac{1}{3}$ cup water into a thick batter. Transfer to a pastry bag fitted with a fine plain tip, and pipe a spiral pattern on the surface of each roll. Bake the rolls in a 400°F (200°C) oven for about 15 minutes, until browned and the spirals are visible. Remove from oven, and brush the rolls with glaze.

The Glaze: Combine the sugar and the gelatin in a small pan with the water and stir over low heat, until the gelatin dissolves and the mixture clears. If you wish, shape a portion of the dough into a wheat stalk. Take one part of the dough and roll it out into a thick strip, 8 inches (20 cm) long. Let rise briefly. With a scissors, make short diagonal cuts alternately on the right and left sides. Let rise in a warm humid place until doubled in bulk. Brush the surface with egg yolk beaten with 1 teaspoon water, and bake in a 400°F (200°C) oven for about 20 minutes, until golden brown. After removing from oven, glaze the surface for a shiny effect.

Preparation time 2 hours and 30 minutes

FOR AN HONORED GUEST

MENU
Avocado Mousse

Spring Prawns with Pasta

Salmon and Sole Terrine
Sauteed Asparagus and Artichokes

Dandelion Greens Salad

Cherry Bavarian Cream or
Raspberry Mousse
Ice Cream Parfait Torte

Chardonnay or Sauvignon Blanc Wine

Avocado Mousse

1	tablespoon unflavored gelatin
4	tablespoons water
2	large ripe avocados
3	tablespoons lemon juice
	a pinch of mashed garlic
15	drops Tabasco sauce
	salt and white pepper, to taste
4	tablespoons finely chopped green onion
1/2	cup heavy cream, whipped
1	jar of brik (red caviar)
	parsley sprigs

Stir the gelatin in water and allow to swell. Place in a double boiler or small pan and stir over low heat until dissolved. Remove from heat, and allow to cool. Peel the avocado, and cut into pieces. Put in a food processor and blend with the lemon juice, Tabasco sauce, garlic, and seasoning at high speed for 1-2 minutes, until smooth. Transfer to a bowl, fold in the gelatin, onion, and whipped cream. Pour the mixture into several small molds, or one shallow mold, grea-sed with corn oil. Refrigerate for several hours, until set. For best results, prepare the day before serving. To serve, unmold the mousse on a platter, top with caviar, and garnish with parsley sprigs. Serve with crackers or melba toast.

Preparation time 30 minutes

Sauce Sabayon

1	cup fish stock
3	egg yolks
1/2	lb (225 gr) cold butter in pats

Use the bones from the fillet of sole (used for the mousseline in Salmon Terrine recipe) to make the fish stock. Simmer until reduced to 5-6 tablespoons. Cool and stir in the egg yolks. Put in a double boiler over hot water and whisk for about 10 minutes, until the mixture is thick. Whisk in the butter pats, a handful at a time, making sure that each addition is completely incorporated into the sauce before the next is added. When enough butter has been incorporated to make a thick, foamy sauce, transfer it to a warmed sauceboat and serve.

Spring Prawns with Pasta

11   oz (300 gr) tagliatelle
5   tablespoons butter or margarine
1/2 cup finely grated onion
2-3 garlic cloves, finely grated
3   lbs (1½ kg) prawns, blanched,
     shelled, and deveined
1½   cup whipping cream
2/3 cup grated Parmesan or
     mild kefalotiri cheese
     salt and pepper, to taste
11   oz (300 gr) broccoli florets,
     blanched

Cook the tagliatelle for about 8 minutes in salted water and drain. Melt 3 tablespoons butter in a large frying pan and lightly saute the onion and garlic. Add the prawns and stir over medium heat, until thoroughly heated. Remove them with a slotted spoon and keep warm in a bowl. Add the rest of the butter and cream into the pan, stirring until the butter melts. Add the Parmesan, salt, and pepper, stir, and pour the mixture over cooked pasta and broccoli. Toss well and transfer to a large serving platter. Arrange the prawns on top and serve immediately.

Preparation time 45 minutes

Brioche Rolls

Prepare brioche dough according to the recipe on page 67. Roll small pieces of dough into strips and shape into pretzels. Or roll into small balls and place in clusters of three to form a cloverleaf pattern. Another variation is to roll out small ovals, and arrange 6 of them joined at the center. When baked, they will resemble daisies. Also you may roll out thick triangles, and starting from the base, roll them up to shape croissants. All suggested shapes are pictured in the bread basket on page 102. Before baking, brush the rolls with an egg yolk beaten with 1 teaspoon water and bake in a 400°F (200°C) oven for 20-25 minutes until golden brown.

Preparation time 3 hours

Salmon and Sole Terrine

1   lb (500 gr) long strips of smoked salmon
2   tablespoons butter
    sauce sabayon

The Mousseline
1   lb (500 gr) boneless fillet of sole
3   egg whites
1½   cups cream
     salt and white pepper, to taste
1/8 teaspoon ground nutmeg
1/8 teaspoon cayenne pepper
1/2 cup coarsely chopped pistachio nuts
1/2 cup pureed spinach

Prepare the mousseline: Puree the sole in a food processor until smooth. Add the egg whites and continue processing, until completely incorporated. Using a plastic scraper, press the mixture gradually through a fine sieve, and discard skins and anything left in the sieve. Place the fish puree in a bowl and press a piece of plastic wrap on the surface. Set in a larger bowl of crushed ice, and refrigerate for at list 1 hour. Using a wooden spoon, work a little of the cream into the puree. Refrigerate for 10 minutes. Continue beating in small quantities of cream, refrigerating for 10 minutes between each addition. If the mixture becomes too soft, stop adding cream, chill and beat vigorously until stiff. When about half the cream has been incorporated, lightly whip the remaining cream and fold into the puree. Refrigerate until ready to use. Fold the pistachio nuts into half the mousseline and season with salt and white pepper. Fold the pureed spinach into the rest and season with nutmeg, cayenne pepper, and salt. Butter an ovenproof loaf pan and line with the smoked salmon strips covering the bottom and sides. Let the ends hang over the rim. Pack the chilled pistachio mousseline in the bottom and cover with the spinach mousseline. Fold in the ends of the fillets. Place the terrine in a larger baking pan, filled with warm water up to half the height of the terrine pan. Bake in a 340°F (175°C) oven for 35-40 minutes, until the surface springs back when pressed. Let stand for a few minutes before tipping the pan carefully to one side to drain the excess juices. Turn the terrine out onto a warm serving platter. Garnish with sauteed white and green asparagus, and artichoke hearts. Serve with sabayon sauce.

Preparation time 4 hours

Dandelion Greens Salad

4¹/₂ lbs (2 kg) dandelion greens, endive,
        beet greens or spinach
1/3   cup olive oil
3   tablespoons lemon juice
        salt and pepper, to taste
        lemon slices for garnish

Trim and wash the greens several times in plenty of cold water. Allow to drain. In a large pot bring ample water to a boil. Add the greens, cover and bring again to a boil over high heat. Lower the heat and simmer for 15-20 minutes until tender. Avoid overcooking. If the greens are too bitter for your taste before completely done, replace the water with fresh boiling water and continue cooking until tender. The greens are more tasty when served warm. If it is not possible to serve them immediately, remove from heat before they are completely done, drain well, and refrigerate. Shortly before serving, place them in boiling water and cook until done. Before serving, mix oil, lemon, salt, and pepper and shake well. Drain the greens, arrange in a shallow serving dish and dress with the oil-lemon sauce. Garnish with lemon slices.

Preparation time 30 minutes

Ice Cream Parfait Torte

2   cups whipping cream
1   teaspoon vanilla extract or 1/2 tsp almond extract
2   cups powdered sugar
10   vanilla wafers or Graham crackers
3   tablespoons Grand Marnier liqueur
8   egg yolks
5   egg whites
4   oz (100 gr) grated semi-sweet
        baking chocolate or chips
1   cup coarsely chopped walnuts
1/2   cup candied or maraschino cherries, quartered
        caramelized walnut halves and
        maraschino cherries for garnish

Whip the cream with four tablespoons of sugar and the vanilla until thick and light. Break the wafers into small pieces, and sprinkle with the liqueur. Beat the egg yolks

with half the remaining sugar until thick and lemon colored. Beat the egg whites in another bowl with the rest of sugar to a soft meringue. Gently fold, first the whipped cream and then the meringue, into the beaten egg yolks, taking care not to deflate the meringue. Fold in the wafers, nuts, quartered cherries and distribute evenly. Empty the mixture into a buttered 10-inch (25-cm) springform pan and freeze. When ready to serve, remove the ring and place the ice cream torte on a serving plate. Garnish with piped whipped cream ribbons, the caramelized walnuts, and maraschino cherries.

Preparation time 1 hour

Raspberry Mousse

2   eggs, separated
1/2 cup sugar
1/4 cup milk
9   oz (250 gr) fresh or frozen raspberries
1   tablespoon unflavored gelatin
2   tablespoons water
1   cup heavy cream, lightly whipped

The Garnish
1   cup heavy cream
2   tablespoons powdered sugar

1/2 teaspoon vanilla extract
    raspberry syrup
    fresh raspberries
    mint leaves

Beat the egg yolks with half the sugar and the milk in a double boiler or small pan, over very low heat, until slightly thickened. Do not boil! Remove from heat. Puree the raspberries in a food processor and fold into the egg yolks. Set aside. Sprinkle the gelatin on the water and allow to swell. Heat until dissolved in a microwave or over hot water. Stir into the raspberry puree mixture. Transfer to a large bowl. Fold in the whipped cream. Beat the egg whites with the remaining sugar to a soft meringue and carefully fold into the raspberry gelatin. Grease 8-10 small clamshell-shaped molds with corn oil and fill with the mousse. Or use one large 10-cup mold. Refrigerate for at least 4 hours, until set. For best results, prepare the day before serving. Lightly whip the cream with sugar and vanilla. Unmold the mousse on dessert plates. Spread some of the whipped cream above the shell on the plate. Pipe the raspberry syrup over the whipped cream in parallel semi-circles, using a fine tip. Starting from the edge of the mousse, draw a skewer, across the raspberry lines, to create the attractive spider's web effect. Garnish with fresh raspberries and mint leaves.

Preparation time 4 hours

146

Cherry Bavarian Cream

1   **cup sugar**
6   **egg yolks**
1   **teaspoon vanilla extract**
3   **cups warm milk**
$1^1/_2$ **tablespoons unflavored gelatin**
4   **tablespoons water**
2   **cups whipping cream**
1   **cup ready-made cherry pie filling**

Beat the sugar and egg yolks in a double boiler, until creamy and lemon-colored. Gradually add the warm milk stirring continuously over low heat, until the custard is thick enough to cover the spoon. Remove from heat and set aside. Sprinkle the gelatin in the water and allow to swell. Heat, until dissolved in a microwave or over hot water. Stir into the hot custard. Cool to lukewarm. Lightly whip the cream with the vanilla and carefully fold into the custard. Grease 6 individual molds with corn oil and fill with the cream. Refrigerate overnight. To serve, unmold onto dessert dishes and garnish with cherry pie filling. To prepare the cherry pie filling see page 175.

Preparation time 45 minutes

Organizing Dinner for an Honored Guest

There are occasions when you are prepared to go all out to entertain someone special. Whether your guest of honor is a professional collegue or a highly regarded personage, you'll want to present a particularly elegant and impressive menu. The recipes suggested in this section will fit your requirements perfectly. Mousse avocado followed by spring prawns with pasta are two attractive starters you can be proud of. The salmon and sole terrine is a truly eclectic main dish guaranteed to tantalize and impress your guest of honor. One of two delicious desserts and an elegant ice cream torte provide a perfect finish to this exceptional meal. Select a fine white wine such as Chardonnay or Sauvignon Blanc to accompany this menu.

❀ *Each recipe serves 6 persons.*
❀ *Well in advance, prepare the rolls, ice cream torte, and the salmon terrine. Store in the freezer.*
❀ *Two days in advance, prepare the Bavarian cream or the raspberry mousse.*
❀ *The day before, trim and wash the dandelion greens and vegetables. Fold the napkins.*
❀ *The evening before, set the table and transfer the terrine from freezer to refrigerator. Make all the preparations for the prawn dish.*
❀ *During the day, saute the vegetables and cook the greens.*
❀ *One hour before serving, put the terrine in the oven, cook the spring prawns, and serve.*

GOLDEN ANNIVERSARY

MENU

Stuffed Celery Boats

Stuffed Eggplant au Gratin

Chicken Cordon Bleu
Vegetable Saute
Cashew-Rice Pilaf

Beet Salad in Aspic

Raisin and Apple Bread Pudding or
Pears with Sabayon Sauce

Chenin Blanc or Rosé Wine

Stuffed Celery Boats

2-3   *celery stalks*
6   *oz (150 gr) smoked salmon*
5   *oz (120 gr) cream cheese*
4   *tablespoons strained yogurt*
1   *tablespoon lemon juice*
1   *tablespoon minced onion*
     salt and pepper, to taste
     red brik and black caviar for garnish

Blend the salmon, cream cheese, yogurt, lemon juice, and onion in a food processor, until the mixture is smooth. Adjust the seasoning and refrigerate. Wash the celery stalks and scrape with a knife pulling off as many of the coarse fibers as you can. Cut each celery stalk into 2-inch (5-cm) lengths. While cutting, destring as described above. Put the salmon mixture in a pastry bag fitted with a large star tip and pipe a garland of smoked salmon into the centers. Garnish half of the celery boats with red brik and half with black caviar. Arrange the celery boats on a platter, cover with plastic wrap, and refrigerate until ready to serve.

Preparation time 20 minutes

Stuffed Eggplant au Gratin

4   *large eggplants*
2   *tablespoons butter*
2   *tablespoons flour*
1/2   *cup milk*
1/2   *cup whipping cream*
1/2   *cup grated mild Kefalotiri cheese*
     salt and pepper, to taste
2   *eggs*

The Topping
1   *cup mashed potatoes or thick bechamel sauce*
1   *egg yolk*
1/4   *cup grated kefalotiri cheese*
     salt and pepper, to taste
1/8   *teaspoon nutmeg*

Wash the eggplant and halve lengthwise. With a sharp knife, score the pulp 3 times lengthwise, making sure not to cut through and damage the skins. Sprinkle liberally with salt and place in a colander for 1 hour. Rinse and lightly squeeze in your hands to remove excess water. Pat dry with paper towels and lightly fry in hot oil. Cool the eggplant and carefully remove most of the pulp with a spoon. Mash with a fork into a coarse puree and set aside. Melt the butter in a

saucepan and saute the flour for 1 minute. Stir in the milk and cream and simmer until the sauce thickens. Remove from heat and cool. Fold in the eggs one at a time, and combine with the eggplant puree, kefalotiri, salt, and freshly ground pepper. Fill the eggplant and arrange in an ovenproof baking dish. Prepare 1 cup thick bechamel or mashed potatoes, and combine with the egg yolk, cheese, pepper, and nutmeg. Transfer to a pastry bag fitted with a large star tip and pipe a zigzag garnish on top of each stuffed eggplant. Bake in a 350°F (180°C) oven for about 30 minutes, until the surface is golden brown. Serve with extra grated kefalotiri.

Preparation time 2 hours

Pinwheel Sesame Rolls

4	cups bread flour
1	tablespoon dry yeast or
1	oz (30 gr) compressed yeast
1½	teaspoon salt
1	tablespoon sugar or honey
2/3	cups lukewarm milk 100°F (40°C)
2	tablespoons melted butter
1	egg
2/3	cup soft butter or margarine

8	oz (250 gr) toasted sesame seeds

Combine dry yeast with the flour in a basin. If using fresh yeast, dissolve in the warm milk and set aside until frothy. Make a well in the center and pour in the rest of the ingredients except for the soft butter and sesame seeds. Gradually taking flour from the sides, mix into a sticky dough. Turn out onto a floured work surface and knead, adding more flour if necessary, until dough is smooth and elastic and no longer sticky. Cover and let rise in a warm, humid place until doubled in bulk. Divide the dough into 4 equal parts. Roll out one part on a well-floured work surface into a rectangle 18x16 inches (20x40 cm). Brush ¼ of the soft butter over the surface and sprinkle lightly with sesame seeds. Roll out the second piece of dough the same size and place it over the first. Brush with ¼ of the soft butter and sprinkle with more sesame seeds. Starting from the long edge, roll up tightly. Cut the roll into pinwheel slices, ³/₄ inch (2 cm) thick. Space well apart on a greased baking sheet, allowing room for expansion while baking. Brush lightly with butter and sprinkle with sesame seeds. Repeat with the other two pieces of dough. Bake in a 400°F (200°C) oven for about 15 minutes, until lightly brown. Cool and freeze until needed.

Preparation time 2 hours and 30 minutes

Chicken Cordon Bleu

4   *large chicken breasts, halved*
1   *cup grated soft Swiss cheese*
1/2 *cup finely chopped ham*
      salt and pepper, to taste
4   *tablespoons prepared mustard*
2   *eggs*
2   *tablespoons olive oil*
1/2 *cup flour*
1/2 *teaspoon salt*
2/3 *cup fine bread crumbs*
      oil for frying

Ask your butcher to flatten the halved breast to about ¼ inch (0.5 cm) thickness. Combine the cheese and ham in a bowl. Season the chicken breasts with salt and freshly ground pepper; spread with mustard. Spoon ⅛ of the cheese and ham mixture on the center of each breast. Fold in short edges and roll up jelly-roll fashion, pressing ends to seal. Secure with toothpicks, if necessary. Refrigerate the rolls until firm. Beat the eggs lightly with the olive oil in a

bowl. Combine ¼ teaspoon salt with the flour. Coat chicken rolls with flour mixture. Dip in egg mixture and roll in bread crumbs. Cover and refrigerate until the crust sets. At this stage the breasts can be frozen. Heat 1-2 inches of vegetable oil in a large frying pan and fry chicken rolls until golden brown. Arrange in an ovenproof baking dish and bake for 15-20 minutes. Serve immediately accompanied by sauteed vegetables and cashew pilaf.

Preparation time 2 hours

Cashew-Rice Pilaf

1/4 *cup butter or margarine*
1/3 *cup finely chopped onion*
1/4 *cup cubed or sliced carrot*
1   *cup long-grain rice*
1/2 *cup wild rice*
2   *cups beef or chicken stock*

1   teaspoon salt
1/2   cup coarsely chopped cashew nuts
1/4   cup finely chopped parsley

Melt the butter in a large pan and saute the onion and carrots until wilted. Add both kinds of rice and stir for 1 minute. Add the hot stock and salt. Cover and simmer for 20-25 minutes, until the rice is tender and the liquid is absorbed. Stir in the cashew nuts and parsley. Serve immediately. If necessary, reheat the pilaf in the microwave, or steam over boiling water.

Preparation time 30 minutes

Vegetable Saute

4   thin leeks, sliced
1   large carrot, thinly sliced
2   celery stalks, thinly sliced
3   tablespoons lemon juice
1/4   cup butter or margarine
      salt and pepper, to taste
2   tablespoons chopped parsley

Melt the butter in a large frying pan and saute the vegetables, stirring at intervals. Add the lemon juice, salt and freshly ground pepper. Cover and simmer for a few minutes, until the liquid is absorbed and the vegetables are glazed. Add the parsley and stir to mix. Serve warm.

Preparation time 20 minutes

Beet Salad in Aspic

2   lbs (1 kg) beet roots
    salt, pepper, vinegar
1   clove garlic, minced
1   tablespoon unflavored gelatin
    curly lettuce leaves and radishes rosettes
    for garnish

Wash and peel the beets. Put in a pan with water to cover and cook until tender. Drain and reserve two cups of the beet juice. Chop the beets into small cubes and place in a bowl. Sprinkle with salt, freshly ground pepper, the minced garlic, and 1/3 of a cup vinegar. Refrigerate overnight. Drain the beets in a colander. Dissolve the gelatin in the reserved beet juice. Chill and when it starts to-gel, stir in the beets. Grease individual molds with corn oil and fill with the beet gelatin. Cover and refrigerate. When ready to serve, arrange the lettuce leaves on a platter. Unmold the aspic on the lettuce and garnish with radish rosettes.

Preparation time 12 hours

Organizing the Golden Anniversary Party

Chicken Cordon Bleu, a celebrated dish for a golden celebration. Few couples indeed have the good fortune to enjoy a golden wedding anniversary. If your parents have been so blessed to have lived together for 50 years, then it is certainly worth the effort to organize a golden anniversary party. Invite a few close friends of their youth. Prepare the famous "blue ribbon chicken" rolls. Extra care and skill are required in the preparation, but we must give due to the modern freezer which allows us to make them long in advance. If melons are in season, carve it into a lovely swan. With the chicken Cordon Bleu, serve Chenin Blanc or Rosé. Accompany the dessert with Champagne.

❀ *Each recipe serves 8 persons.*
❀ *Well in advance prepare the sesame rolls, bread pudding, and chicken cordon bleu. Store in the freezer.*
❀ *The morning before, prepare the beets in aspic, clean and cut the celery boats. Prepare the salmon filling. Cover and refrigerate each separately. Prepare the pears up to the stage specified in the recipe, and refrigerate.*
❀ *The afternoon before, prepare and fill the eggplant; refrigerate.*
❀ *The evening before, set the table.*
❀ *In the morning, remove pre-prepared dishes from the freezer.*
❀ *In the afternoon, prepare the pilaf and the vegetables. Fill the celery boats and fry the chicken rolls.*
❀ *Thirty minutes before serving, bake the stuffed eggplant.*
❀ *As soon as the eggplants have been served, start baking the chicken.*

Raisin and Apple Bread Pudding

12	slices soft white bread (crusts removed)
6	tablespoons soft butter
1/2	cup white raisins, rinsed and dried
1	large apple, thinly sliced
1	tablespoon lemon juice
8	eggs
2/3	cups sugar
2	cups whipping cream
2	cups milk
1/2	teaspoon cinnamon or lemon zest
1	teaspoon vanilla
	custard or fruit sauce for serving

Butter the slices of bread, arrange on a baking sheet and bake in a 350°F (180°C) oven for about 15 minutes, until lightly toasted. Meanwhile lightly beat the eggs with the sugar. While beating continuously, add the milk, cream and flavorings. Butter a medium-deep, round ovenproof baking dish and place 4 pieces of toast on the bottom, spaced well apart. Sprinkle with ⅓ of the raisins. While slicing the apple, sprinkle with lemon juice to prevent discoloration. Spread ⅓ of the apple slices over the raisins and gradually spoon over ⅓ of the egg mixture. Allow time for the toast to absorb the liquid and repeat the procedure twice with the rest of the ingredients. Cover and let stand for 1 hour until the toast swells. At this stage, you can freeze the pudding. When ready to serve, thaw out completely. To bake, place the pudding in a larger pan filled with water up to half the height of the dish. Bake in a 340°F (175°C) oven for about 1 hour. If the surface starts to burn, cover the dish with aluminum foil. Serve while still lukewarm accompanied by custard sauce (page 44) or a fruit sauce (apple, strawberry, or raspberry) (page 55).

Preparation time 1 hour and 30 minutes

Pears with Sabayon Sauce

8	firm pears about the same size
1/2	cup sugar
1½	cups water
1/2	cup white wine
4	tablespoons julienned orange and lemon peel
1	cinnamon stick
6	cloves

The Sauce

3	*egg yolks*
3	*tablespoons sugar*
1	*cup white wine, champagne, or sherry*
1/4	*teaspoon vanilla extract*

Peel the pears, leaving the stems intact. Place upright, side by side into a pan that will just take them. In a separate pan, stir the water with the sugar over medium heat, until completely dissolved. Add the wine, peel, cinnamon, and cloves. Bring to a boil and pour it over the pears. Cover and simmer for 10-15 minutes, until tender. Remove the pears with a slotted spoon. Strain the liquid through a sieve and discard the cinnamon stick and cloves. Boil the liquid and reduce, until thick enough to cover a spoon. Pour the syrup over the pears. Cover with plastic wrap and refrigerate. To prepare the Sabayon sauce, beat the egg yolks with the sugar in a double boiler over low heat until the sugar dissolves and the mixture is thick and creamy. Gradually add the wine, beating continuously. The mixture will gradually become more white and frothy; in about 5 minutes it will have doubled in bulk. Beat for an additional 5-10 minutes. Serve warm, or place the container in a bowl of ice and stir until it cools. It can de served either way. This sauce is an excellent accompaniment for fresh fruit, preserves, cakes, tarts, soufflés, or puddings. You may use canned pear halves instead of fresh. Drain and arrange on a plate with the cut surface down and pour the Sabayon sauce over them.

Preparation time 30 minutes

NAME DAY CELEBRATION

MENU

Cheese Croquettes or
Stuffed Artichoke Hearts

Lasagne al Forno or
Meat Loaf

Lamb with Onion Sauce
Potato and Carrot Puree

Festive Salad

Ice Cream Brownie Torte or
Walnut and Kiwi Gâteau

«Agioritiko» Mount Athos Wine
White or Rosé

Cheese Croquettes

1½   *lbs (700 gr) grated kasseri or pecorino cheese*
3   *egg whites, lightly beaten*
1/4   *teaspoon white pepper*
      corn oil for frying

Combine the cheese with the beaten egg whites and white pepper in a bowl. Refrigerate until the mixture is thick and pliable. If too soft and sticky, add more grated cheese until the mixture can be shaped into little balls. At this stage cheese croquettes can be frozen; or keep refrigerated until ready to use. Fry in hot corn oil, turning over until all sides are golden brown. Remove with a slotted spoon and drain on paper towels. Serve hot.

Preparation time 30 minutes

Stuffed Artichoke Hearts

3   *lbs (1½ kg) canned artichoke hearts (18 pieces)*

The Filling
7   *oz (200 gr) cream cheese*
5   *oz (140 gr) Camembert cheese*
4   *oz (100 gr) grated Romano cheese*
1   *teaspoon dried herbs, such as thyme, mint,*
      parsley, basil, tarragon
      salt and pepper, to taste
1/2   *teaspoon paprika*

Rinse the artichokes and thoroughly drain. With your fingers, open each one slightly at the center. Remove the centers with a teaspoon. Trim tough outer leaves with a scissors so artichokes are the same size. Drain on paper towels. Combine all the filling ingredients and stuff the artichoke centers, pushing in as much filling as possible. At this stage they can be frozen; or keep refrigerated until ready to serve. Brush lightly with melted margarine and arrange on a greased baking sheet. Bake in a 340°F (175°C) oven for about 20 minutes, until the tops are golden brown. Serve hot.

Preparation time 45 minutes

Lasagne al Forno

1/4	cup olive oil
1/4	cup grated onion
1	small carrot, grated
1	celery stalk, finely chopped
1	lb (450 gr) ground beef
1/3	cup white wine
	salt and pepper, to taste
2	lbs (900 gr) fresh or
	canned tomatoes, pulped
1	can 1 lb (450 gr) tomato juice
1/4	cup butter
2	tablespoons flour
1½	cups hot milk
4	oz (100 gr) grated Emmentaler cheese
4	oz (100 gr) grated Parmesan
1	lb (450 gr) lasagne noodles
1	lb (450 gr) shredded mozzarella

Heat the oil in a pan and saute the onions, carrots, and celery until wilted. Add the ground meat and stir over high heat, until all juices are absorbed. Add the wine, salt, and freshly ground pepper. Cook over high heat, until the wine evaporates. Add tomatoes and tomato juice, cover, and simmer until the sauce thickens. Remove from heat and cool. Meanwhile, melt the butter in a saucepan, and saute the flour for 1 minute. Add the milk, and stirring vigorously, simmer until the bechamel thickens. Add the Emmentaler and Parmesan, stir briefly over heat until the cheeses melt. Remove from heat and set aside. Bring ample salted water to a boil in a large pot with 3 tablespoons olive oil. Cook the lasagne noodles a few at a time, about 4 minutes until softened. Remove with slotted spoon and plunge into another pot filled with cold water, to cool until they can be handled. Drain the lasagne noodles and dry on paper towels. Generously butter a large, ovenproof lasagne dish 14x16 inches (35x40 cm). Cover the bottom with lasagne noodles, and spread with meat sauce, bechamel, and mozzarella. Repeat with 4 more layers of lasagne, meat sauce, bechamel, and cheese. At this stage, the dish may be frozen. When ready to serve, thaw out first and bake in a 350°F (180°C) oven for about 35 minutes, until well browned. Remove from oven and allow to cool for 5 minutes before cutting into squares and serving.

Preparation time 3 hours

Meat Loaf

The Filling
1	can sliced mushrooms 30 oz (800 gr)
1/2	cup grated onion
1/4	cup flour
1	cup hot milk
1/2	cup whipping cream
2	egg yolks
1/2	cup grated mild kefalotiri cheese
1/8	teaspoon allspice
1/4	cup finely chopped parsley

The Meat Mixture
3	lbs (1½ kg) ground beef
2/3	cup grated stale bread (crust removed)
1/4	cup grated onion
1/3	cup ketchup
2	egg whites
2/3	cup meat stock
1/2	teaspoon ginger
1/2	teaspoon coriander
1/2	teaspoon thyme
	salt and pepper, to taste
	grated kefalotiri cheese

The Filling: Drain the canned mushrooms in a colander and discard the liquid. Heat the butter in a saucepan and saute the mushrooms and onions, until wilted. Add the flour and cook 2 minutes. Stirring vigorously, add the hot milk, and cook, stirring over low heat until the sauce thickens. Add the cream and cook briefly. Remove from heat and fold in the egg yolk, cheese, herbs, spices, salt, and freshly ground pepper. Set aside.

The Meat Mixture: Combine the ingredients in a bowl. Gradually adding enough stock, knead to a smooth and uniform mixture. Pat ³⁄₄ of the meat mixture into the bottom and sides of a greased double meatloaf mold, or a simple loaf pan 10x6x2.5 inches (24x16x6 cm). Pour ²⁄₃ of the filling into the lined mold. Pat the remaining meat mixture into a rectangle the same dimensions as the top of mold, and cover the filling. Pinch the edges of the meat together, sealing the filling in. Sprinkle grated kefalotiri on top. Bake in a 340°F (175°C) oven for 1 hour and 15 minutes. Remove from oven and cool. If using a meat loaf mold, lift out the inside of the mold to drain the meat loaf, then turn out onto a platter. If using a simple loaf pan, carefully tip it to one side to drain the excess juices before unmolding onto a platter. Pour the remaining ¹⁄₃ of the mushroom filling over the meatloaf. Serve hot.

Preparation time 1 hour and 30 minutes

Lamb with Onion Sauce

3   lbs (1½ kg) spring lamb, cut into serving portions
1/4 cup olive oil or butter
4   large onions, grated
     salt and pepper, to taste
1   egg
1/4 cup lemon juice
1   French baguette, sliced
1/4 cup soft butter
1   pimento, for the garnish

Wash and trim the meat, removing as much fat as possible. Drain and pat dry on paper towels. Heat the oil in a large pan and lightly brown the meat. Add the onions and saute over medium heat until liquid is absorbed and onions are transparent. Add salt, freshly ground pepper, and ¹⁄₂ cup of water. Cover and simmer until the meat is tender. Remove the meat with a fork and set aside. Pour the onion sauce from the pot into a food processor and blend for 1 minute, until thick and light-colored. Return the meat and the sauce into the pot, and slowly bring to a boil. Lightly beat the eggs with the lemon juice in a bowl and gradually add a few tablespoons of the hot onion sauce, continuously beating. Pour the tempered egg-lemon mixture slowly into the simmering food and shake the pan gently, to blend the sauce. Remove from heat. To serve, arrange the lamb portions on a metal platter. Pour some of the sauce over them, and serve the rest in a gravy boat. Garnish the lamb with pimento. Butter both sides of bread slices, and toast in a non-stick frypan over medium heat, on both sides until golden brown. Arrange around the outer edge of the platter.

Preparation time 2 hours

Potato and Carrot Puree

2   lbs (900 gr) potatoes
1   lb (450 gr) carrots
1/2 cup milk
1/2 cup whipping cream
1/4 cup butter
     salt and white pepper, to taste
1/8 teaspoon nutmeg (optional)
8   oz (240 gr) broccoli florets, cooked

Peel the potatoes and carrots and cut into pieces. In separate pans, boil the potatoes and carrots with just enough water to cook them and be absorbed. Mash the carrots and potatoes together and pass through a food mill. Add cream, butter, and enough milk; whip to make a puree stiff enough to retain its shape. Add salt, white pepper, and nutmeg, if desired. Place the puree in a pastry bag fitted with a large star tip and pipe large rosettes on a round platter. Garnish with cooked broccoli florets and miniature animal shapes cut out from carrots.

Preparation time 45 minutes

Festive Salad

2   cups grated carrot
2   cups grated cabbage
2   cups grated red cabbage
1   large white radish, thinly sliced
     pieces of canned pimento
2   Belgian endive (chicory)

On a large round platter, arrange both kinds of grated cabbage and the grated carrot in three concentric circles. Roll the sliced white radish into cones and secure with wooden toothpicks. Place in cold water for 2 hours. Remove the toothpicks, arrange the radish cones at the center of the salad with a small piece of pimento inside each. Surround the salad with endive leaves, pointing out like rays. Just before serving, sprinkle the salad with salt and freshly ground pepper and dress with oil and lemon, two parts oil to one part lemon.

Preparation time 30 minutes

Festive Bread

4½   cups bread flour
1   tablespoon dry yeast
2   teaspoons salt
2   tablespoons sugar
3   tablespoons melted butter
1½   cups lukewarm milk 100°F (40°C)
1   cup coarsely chopped walnuts
2   egg yolks, beaten with 2 teaspoons water
2   tablespoons sesame seeds
2   tablespoons onion seeds
2   tablespoons paprika
2   tablespoons anise
2   tablespoons coarsely chopped almonds

Combine the yeast, salt and sugar with the flour in the large mixing bowl of an electric mixer. Combine the butter and milk and pour into the bowl. Knead the mixture with the dough hook at low speed for 8-10 minutes. Cover the dough and let rise in a warm, humid place until doubled in bulk. Punch the dough down, cut and set aside ¼ of it. Roll out the remaining dough into a thick rectangle, sprinkle with walnuts and roll up. Divide into 5 equal parts and shape into balls. Arrange them side by side next to each other in a greased round shallow baking tin. With the reserved dough, roll out 5 long, thin strips fold in half and twist. Arrange the twists over the points where the 5 sections of dough meet, from the center to the edges. Brush them lightly with beaten egg yolk, so they will stick in place when baking. Cover with a cloth and allow the loaf to rise until doubled in bulk. Brush the entire surface with beaten egg yolk and sprinkle each section separately with one of the 5 different spices, seeds or nuts. Bake the loaf in a 400°F (200°C) oven for 20-25 minutes, until golden brown.   Preparation time 3 hours

Ice Cream Brownie Torte

The Base
3   oz (80 gr) semi-sweet baking chocolate
1/3   cup unsalted butter, margarine, or corn oil
2   eggs
3/4   cup sugar
3/4   cup all-purpose flour
1   teaspoon baking powder
1/2   teaspoon vanilla extract
3/4   cup coarsely chopped walnuts

The Filling
2   lbs (1 kg) vanilla ice cream
7   oz (200 gr) whipped cream
8   strawberries
1   recipe chocolate sauce (page 165)

Melt the baking chocolate with the butter in a double boiler. Cool slightly; add the vanilla, then the eggs one at a time, stirring vigorously. Set aside. Sift the flour with the baking powder. Fold sugar and flour mixture into the melted chocolate. Stir in the walnuts. Line two 10-inch (26-cm) round shallow baking pans with non-stick baking paper. Spread half of the mixture into each pan. Bake in a 340°F (175°C) oven for about 20 minutes. Remove from oven and cool on wire racks. Place one of the brownie bases on a round platter and spread with softened ice cream. Place the second brownie base on top and press lightly with your hands. Cover with plastic wrap and freeze. When ready to serve, garnish with whipped cream and strawberries. Accompany with chocolate sauce served in a sauce boat.

Preparation time 45 minutes

Walnut and Kiwi Gâteau

The Sponge
4   large eggs
1/2   cup sugar
1   cup ground walnuts
1/3   cup self-rising flour
1   tablespoon cocoa
1/4   cup melted unsalted butter

The Custard
1/4   cup cornstarch
1/3   cup sugar
1   teaspoon vanilla extract
5   egg yolks
1½   cups hot milk

The Garnish
2   tablespoons brandy
14   oz (400 gr) whipped cream
6   large kiwis, sliced crosswise
1/2   lb (225 gr) raspberries or strawberries

Beat the eggs and sugar with an electric mixer at high speed for about 15 minutes, until thick and creamy. Sift the flour with the cocoa. Stirring gently, gradually fold a tablespoon at a time into the beaten eggs. Stir in the walnuts and the melted butter, a tablespoon at a time, taking care not to deflate the eggs. Line two 10-inch (25-cm) round baking pans with non-stick baking paper. Pour half the mixture into each pan. Bake the sponges in a 350°F (180°C) oven for about 35 minutes. Meanwhile, prepare the custard. Combine the cornstarch and sugar in a saucepan. Add the egg yolks and vanilla. Whisk, until thick and foamy. Pour in the hot milk, stirring vigorously and cook over low heat, until the custard is thick and smooth. Cool completely and fold in 1 cup of whipped cream. Place one sponge on a platter, sprinkle with half the brandy and spread with the custard. Place the second sponge on top, sprinkle with the rest of brandy, and frost with a thin layer of whipped cream. Place the remaining whipped cream in a pastry bag and garnish the gâteau with garlands and rosettes. Arrange the sliced kiwi and the raspberries or strawberry halves on top of the gâteau. Cover with plastic wrap and refrigerate until ready to serve.

Preparation time 1 hour and 15 minutes

Chocolate Sauce

4   oz (100 gr) semi-sweet baking chocolate or chips
1/3 cup whipping cream
**   a few drops of vanilla extract**

Put the chocolate pieces in a small heavy pan. Add the cream and vanilla and stir over low heat until the chocolate melts and the sauce coats the spoon. Take care not to overheat or burn the sauce.

Organizing a "Name Day Celebration"

In many countries a Name Day is celebrated on the day the church honors the saint of the same name. According to tradition, name days are marked with a festive meal for the family at midday. In the evening, open house is held for other relatives and friends who come to bring their best wishes. The tasty dishes in this menu were selected as appropriate for a gathering of the whole family. The table settings are designed to create the proper festive atmosphere for this special day. For an elegant touch to the occasion, tastefully decorate the table with flowers, candles, and crystal on fine linen. White porcelain china and silverware are set off with napkins folded like water lilies with a fresh flower in the center. Mount Athos (Agioritiko) white or rosé wine is a good choice for this occasion. This famous regional Greek wine comes from special grape varieties cultivated by monks in Mount Athos.

❀   *Each recipe serves 8 persons.*

❀   *Well in advance prepare the lasagne or meat loaf, the cheese croquettes, festive bread, and ice cream torte. Store in the freezer.*

❀   *Two days in advance, make the gâteau without the garnishes. Peel and clean the vegetables. Keep refrigerated.*

❀   *The evening before, fix the salad, garnish the gâteau, and stuff the artichokes. Refrigerate. Transfer the lasagne to the refrigerator. Set the table.*

❀   *During the day, remove the bread from the freezer and let thaw. Cook the lamb, make the potato and carrot puree.*

❀   *One hour before serving, place the lasagne in the oven.*

❀   *Just before serving, fry the croquettes and bake the stuffed artichokes. "Chronia Polla" (Many Happy Returns).*

FESTIVE HOLIDAY GATHERING

MENU

*Shrimp Salad in Endive or
Yuletide Appetizer Tree*

❧

Sole and Spinach Soufflé

❧

Chicken Milanese

❧

Holiday Cheese Board

❧

Christmas Bread Wreath

❧

*Festive Fruit Trifle
Puff Pastry Stars
Meringue Hearts and Wreaths*

❧

Chardonnay Fumé Wine

Shrimp Salad in Endive

The Salad
1	cup cooked baby shrimp
2	tablespoons finely chopped fresh dill
2	tablespoons finely chopped red bell pepper
2	tablespoons finely chopped green pepper
2	tablespoons chopped green onion
2	tablespoons finely chopped fresh mushrooms
2	tablespoons corn kernels
1/4	cup finely chopped cucumber
2-3	tablespoons mayonnaise
1	teaspoon lemon juice
1	teaspoon prepared mustard
5-6	drops Tabasco sauce
	salt and pepper, to taste

The Garnish
2	Belgian endives
	parsley leaves
2	radish rosettes

Separate the Belgian endives into leaves, wash and drain in a colander. Combine the first 8 ingredients in a bowl.

In another bowl, combine the mayonnaise with the rest of the ingredients and stir, until smooth. Toss the shrimp salad with this dressing and fill the endive leaves. Arrange them on a platter like petals of two large daisies with the radish rosettes on a bed of parsley at the centers. Cover with plastic wrap and refrigerate until ready to serve.

Preparation time 20 minutes

Sole and Spinach Soufflé

2	lbs (1 kg) spinach
1/4	cup butter or margarine
1/2	cup finely chopped green onions
1/4	cup finely chopped parsley
	salt and pepper, to taste
3	cups grated mild kefalotiri or Swiss cheese
4	eggs, separated
2	cups whipping cream
1	small carrot
1	small onion

3-4   *parsley sprigs*
1   *bay leaf*
1   *garlic clove*
20   *peppercorns*
3   *lbs (1½ kg) boneless fillet of sole*
5   *tablespoons butter or margarine*
5   *tablespoons flour*
1/8 *teaspoon nutmeg*
      parsley and pimento
      for garnish

Wash and trim the spinach; chop and blanch. Drain and squeeze out excess water, pressing between palms. Heat the butter in a saucepan and saute the onions. Add spinach and stir over high heat for a few minutes. Remove from heat and set aside to cool. Add parsley, 1 cup grated cheese, salt, and freshly ground pepper. Beat the egg whites with 1 cup cream in a bowl and stir half of it into the spinach mixture. Butter a large ovenproof dish and sprinkle with bread crumbs. Spread the spinach mixture over the bottom. Bring 2 cups water to a boil with the carrot, onion, parsley, bay leaf, garlic, and 20 peppercorns. Add the fillet of sole and cook for 5 minutes. Strain and reserve the stock, about 2 cups. Skin and flake the sole. Combine with 1 cup grated cheese and the remaining beaten egg white and cream

mixture. Season with salt and freshly ground pepper. Spread the fish mixture over the spinach in the dish. Melt the butter in a small saucepan, add the flour and saute 1-2 minutes. Stir in the reserved fish stock and simmer until the sauce thickens. Remove from heat, add the nutmeg, a pinch of salt, and white pepper. Cool briefly. Meanwhile, beat the egg yolks with the rest of cream and fold into the sauce along with the remaining cheese. Spread the sauce over the fish. At this stage the soufflé may be frozen. To cook, remove from the freezer and allow the soufflé to thaw out. Dot the surface with butter, and bake in a 350°F (180°C) oven for 45-60 minutes, until the top is golden brown. Before serving, garnish the top with a wreath of parsley leaves, and a ribbon of pimento tied in a bow.

Preparation time 2 hours

Chicken Milanese

1	whole chicken and 3 breasts
7½	cups water
1/2	cup butter or margarine
1	small onion
20	peppercorns
2	teaspoons salt
2	cups long-grain rice

The Velouté Sauce
1/4	cup butter or margarine
3	tablespoons flour
2	cups warm chicken stock
	salt and white pepper, to taste
2	tablespoons lemon juice

The Garnish
cooked broccoli florets
pimento stars
parsley sprigs

Skin the chicken and halve the breasts. Place in a large pan

with the water and the rest of the ingredients except for the rice. Cover and simmer until the meat is tender. Remove the chicken with a slotted spoon. Separate, cover, and keep the 8 breast halves warm. Debone the rest of the chicken and finely chop. Strain the stock through a fine sieve and measure. Add water, if necessary, to measure 7 cups. Using 5 cups of stock, cook the rice. When the rice is ready, mix with the finely chopped chicken. Pack into a buttered tube cake pan, cover and keep warm.

Prepare the velouté sauce: Melt the butter in a heavy saucepan, over medium heat and stir in the flour for 2-3 minutes, until it is light golden. Stirring vigorously, add the remaining chicken stock and cook until the sauce thickens. Remove from heat and cool slightly. Add the lemon juice, white pepper, and salt if needed. When ready to serve, unmold the rice on a large round platter and surround with chicken breasts and broccoli florets. Dribble the sauce over the tops. To garnish, top the pilaf with the pimento stars, and the breasts with small parsley sprigs.

Preparation time 2 hours and 30 minutes

Christmas Bread Wreath

1   *oz (30 gr) fresh yeast or*
1   *tablespoon dry yeast*
4   *cups bread flour*
1¹⁄₂ *teaspoons salt*
1/4 *cup lukewarm water 100°F (40°C)*
3/4 *cup lukewarm milk 100°F (40°C)*
1   *egg*
2   *tablespoons sugar*
1/2 *cup melted margarine*
3   *tablespoons finely chopped red bell pepper*
3   *tablespoons finely chopped green pepper*
1/2 *cup grated kefalotiri cheese*
1/4 *teaspoon paprika*

Dissolve the yeast in water with 2 tablespoons flour and let rise for 10 minutes. Sift the flour with the salt in a large bowl, and make a well in the center. Pour in the milk, egg, sugar, half the margarine, and the yeast. Gradually taking the flour from the sides, mix with the liquid until a soft, sticky dough is formed. Turn out onto a well-floured work surface and knead, adding as much flour as needed until the dough is smooth and elastic and no longer sticky. Cover and let rise in a warm, humid place until doubled in bulk, 1-2 hours. Meanwhile, pour the rest of melted margarine into the bottom of a 1-quart ring mold and sprinkle chopped red and green pepper. Combine kefalotiri and paprika in a bowl. On a well-floured worktop, roll out the dough into a long, thick roll and divide into 24 equal pieces. Dip one cut side of each piece of dough in the grated cheese. Stand pieces on edge, slightly overlapping, in prepared mold. Sprinkle any remaining kefalotiri on top. Cover with a cloth and let the bread rise in a warm humid place until doubled in bulk. Bake the loaf in a 350°F (180°C) oven for 25-30 minutes, until golden brown. Remove from oven, loosen edges, and invert onto a wire rack. Cool to room temperature and transfer to a plate. The bread ring can be frozen until ready to serve. When thawed out, it will be as fresh and light as at the moment you took it out of the oven. Decorate with a red bow and holly.

Preparation time 3 hours and 30 minutes

Yuletide Appetizer Tree

Completely cover a styrofoam cone with curly endive, pinning the leaves on with toothpicks. Using decorative wooden hors d'oeuvre sticks, pin a crown of radish rosettes on top of the cone. Wash, wipe, and slice a few large mushrooms and a couple of small cucumbers. Make long, thin, carrot ribbons with a potato peeler, and shape them into rolls. Pin the vegetables to the cone in alternating rows. Also you can use cauliflower florets, cherry tomatoes, or celery slices. Serve the crudités with two or three dippers.

Yogurt Dip: Blend $3/4$ cup strained yogurt, $1/4$ cup cream, 1 tablespoon finely chopped green onion, 1 tablespoon lemon juice, and 1 teaspoon sugar in a food processor, until smooth.

Hot Tomato Dip: In 1 tablespoon olive oil, saute 1 tablespoon grated onion and 1 small minced clove of garlic, until wilted. Add 1 small crushed chili pepper, or $1/4$ chili powder, 1 teaspoon dry marjoram, 1 tablespoon brown sugar, $1/4$ cup dry red wine, and $1^1/2$ cups chopped tomatoes. Cover and simmer until the sauce thickens. Cool and refrigerate.

Cream Cheese Dip: Blend 4 oz (120 gr) cream cheese, 1 cup sour cream, 1 tablespoon chili sauce, and a pinch of dried mint in a food processor to a smooth mixture.

Preparation time 1 hour and 30 minutes

Holiday Cheese Board

With miniature Christmas cookie cutters, cut bite-sized pieces out of different kinds of cheese (Emmentaler, mozzarella, smoked cheese, Cheddar, Swiss or kefalotiri). Blend blue cheese with a bit of cream cheese, form into little balls, and roll in coarsely chopped paprika. Arrange the cheeses in rows on a wooden cheese platter, with rows of radish stars, grapes, and small whole strawberries, or other little fruits which complement the flavors of the cheeses. At the top of the board, place a grapefruit decorated with little "shooting" stars cut from red, green, and yellow bell pepper. To make the rays of the shooting-stars, cut the white part of green onions into 2-inch (4-cm) lengths. Using a sharp knife or scissors, start at one end and score them lengthwise, stopping short of the other end. Place in cold water to open. Impale them on thin bamboo skewers with pepper stars at one end and stick into the grapefruit.

Preparation time 45 minutes

Meringue Hearts and Wreaths

2   **egg whites**
1/4 **teaspoon cream of tartar**
1/2 **cup sugar**
      red and green food coloring
      almond extract, mint extract

Beat the egg whites and cream of tartar with the mixer at high speed, until foamy. While beating, gradually add the sugar, until the meringue holds stiff peaks. Divide into 2 parts. Add 2-3 drops red food coloring and $^1/_8$ teaspoon vanilla or almond extract into one part of meringue and 2-3 drops green food coloring and $^1/_8$ teaspoon peppermint extract to the other part. Gently mix to blend in the colors. Draw little hearts and circles on baking paper. Fill two separate pastry bags with the tinted meringues. Using a star-shaped tip, pipe ribbons following the lines onto the baking paper, and shape green wreaths and pink hearts. Sprinkle the meringues with fine, colored-sugar decors. Dry them in a 165°F (80°C) oven with the fan on, for about 2 hours. Turn off the heat and let them cool in the oven. Carefully pull off the baking paper, and store them in an airtight tin. Properly stored, the meringues will keep for up to 6 months.

Preparation time 2 hours and 30 minutes

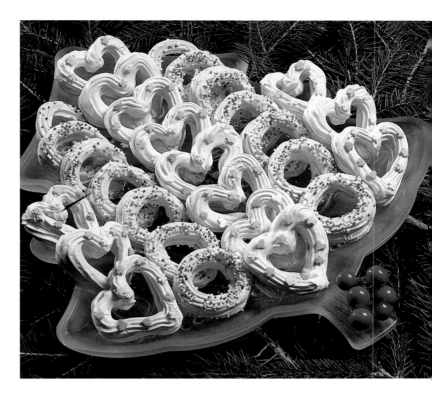

Organizing your Festive Holiday Gathering

Share the joy and magic of the Holiday Season by inviting your friends to a table laden with irresistible homemade treats. Good food enjoyed in the company of good friends is one of life's greatest pleasures. The menu recommended here is full of special holiday recipes and decoration ideas which are sure to put you and everyone around you in the holiday mood. Create a festive holiday atmosphere in your home and at the dinner table with the following: Fold the napkins into candles, and put a poinsettia in each one. Put a red candle in ice, and put it in the window or corner of the holiday buffet. Make a "wreath" of bread and some pastry "stars". Holiday gift sweets baked and given with love show how much you care. The dishes in this menu call for demi-sec wine such as Sauvignon Fumé. Also you can splurge by serving Champagne with dessert.

❀ *Each recipe serves 8 persons.*
❀ *Late in November, prepare the sole and spinach soufflé, the bread wreath, cherry sauce, meringues, pastry stars, and gift cakes (without frosting or garnishes) , and store as specified in the recipes.*
❀ *The morning before, prepare the cheese board, vegetables for the salads, and dippers for the appetizers.*
❀ *The afternoon before, make the trifle, mix the shrimp salad in a bowl, and refrigerate. Remove the soufflé from the freezer to the refrigerator.*
❀ *The evening before, set and decorate the table.*
❀ *In the morning, remove the pastry stars and the bread from the freezer. Decorate the cheese platter and appetizer tree. Cover with plastic wrap and refrigerate or store in a cool place.*
❀ *In the afternoon, prepare the chicken Milanese and stuff the endive with the shrimp salad.*
❀ *One hour before serving, bake the soufflé.*

173

Puff Pastry Stars

1   lb puff pastry (in 2 large sheets)
1   lb (450 gr) cream cheese, softened
2/3 cups sugar
2   eggs
1   teaspoon vanilla extract
2   cups cherry sauce (page 175)

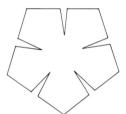

8   oz (250 gr) whipping cream
2   tablespoons powdered sugar
1   teaspoon vanilla extract

Beat the cream cheese with the sugar, eggs and vanilla in a bowl, until mixed. On a well-floured worktop, open the pastry sheets. Using a cardboard cutout as a guide, cut each sheet into 6 pentagons with 3.5-inch (9-cm) sides. Place on 2 buttered baking sheets. At the center of each side make a 1.5-inch cut from the edge towards the center. Put 3 tablespoons of cheese filling onto the center and spread towards the corners. Starting at one corner, bring up 2 adjacent sides; overlap to form point. Wet sides and press lightly to seal. Repeat with remaining corners, to form a 5-pointed star. Brush with a little melted butter. If you have a convection oven you can bake them all together in a 400°F (200°C) oven for 15-20 minutes. Otherwise, bake one sheet at a time. Because puff pastry expands better when baked cold, refrigerate the pastries for 2 hours before baking. After baking, cool on a rack. Meanwhile, make the cherry sauce according to the recipe on page 175. Whip the cream with the powdered sugar and vanilla. Put in a pastry bag fitted with a large star tip and chill until ready to use. Put 2 tablespoons cherry sauce in the center of each pastry. Pipe a wreath of whipped cream around the cherries. Refrigerate until ready to serve.

Preparation time 2 hours

Cherry Sauce

Various canned fruit sauces (pie fillings) are available on the market. To make homemade cherry sauce, drain and measure the juice from a 28 oz (800 gr) can of cherries. For each cup of juice, add two tablespoons of cornstarch (and two tablespoons sugar if the juice is not sweet). Stir over low heat until thick and clear. Remove from heat, stir in $1/8$ teaspoon almond extract, and the cherries. Cool to room temperature before using.

Festive Fruit Trifle

5   oz (150 gr) ladyfingers
1/2   cup sherry
1   cup raspberry or strawberry jam
10   kiwis, peeled and sliced into rounds
20   large strawberries, cut in half lengthwise
1/2   cup coarsely chopped blanched
       almonds or walnuts
2   cups heavy cream, whipped

The Custard
9   egg yolks
1/2   cup sugar
3   cups hot milk
1   teaspoon vanilla extract

Prepare the custard: Beat the egg yolks with sugar and vanilla in a double boiler until thick. Add hot milk and continue stirring over simmering water, until the mixture thickens enough to coat a spoon. Remove from heat and immediately immerse the pan in cold water, to stop cooking and prevent curdling. The custard thickens as it cools. Alternatively, use ready-to-mix custard powder or cornstarch with at least 3 cups of milk. Follow directions on package.
Assemble the trifle: In a large, deep glass bowl, arrange $1/3$ of the ladyfingers and sprinkle with 2 tablespoons sherry. Spread them with $1/3$ cup of jam using a spatula and sprinkle 2 tablespoons of nuts on top. Cover with $1/3$ of the custard. Arrange a row of kiwi fruit slices around the edge of the bowl, and cut the remaining in quarters. Reserve about 20 and spread the rest over the custard. Lay half the remaining ladyfingers on top, sprinkle with 2 tablespoons sherry and spread with half the remaining jam. Sprinkle 3 tablespoons nuts and cover with half the remaining custard. Arrange some of the strawberry halves, upright, around the edge of the bowl. Reserve 10 strawberry halves and spread the rest over the custard. For the final 3 layers, arrange the remaining ladyfingers (sprinkled with the rest of the sherry), the remaining marmalade, nuts, and cover with the rest of the custard. Garnish the top of the trifle with rosettes of whipped cream between rows of kiwi and strawberries. Refrigerate until ready to serve.
Alternatively: Other seasonal fruits, jams or preserves can be substituted for the kiwi and strawberries, according to their availability or your preference.

Preparation time 1 hour

175

Sweet Holiday Gifts

This is the season of giving. Delight your relatives and friends with beautiful homemade Holiday goodies. Prepare your favorite yellow cake and garnish with green candied fruits and small red sugar candies. Put a red ribbon on top to make the cake look like a wreath. Or bake the cake in a tree-shaped mold (page 174) and trim with green glaze and colored sugar candies. Crown the tree with a star or a red poinsettia. To make a coconut cake, use your regular white cake recipe, substituting 1 cup flaked coconut for 1 cup flour. Frost with whipped cream, and sprinkle shredded coconut all over to resemble newly fallen snow. Draw evergreen trees on a sheet of waxed paper and outline with melted chocolate using a pastry bag fitted with narrow plain tip. Refrigerate until the chocolate hardens. Carefully remove the chocolates from the paper and stand upright around the coconut cake. Another idea is to make a chocolate cake baked in a metal mixing bowl. Unmold on a round plate and frost with white icing. Garnish with green shredded coconut and little chocolate bells. For the bows use red licorice. To make the bells, melt 5 oz (125 gr) semi-sweet baking chocolate with 1 tablespoon corn oil in a saucepan, and spread on a baking sheet covered with waxpaper. Refrigerate until the chocolate hardens. Cut out bells, trees, stars with Christmas cookie cutters. Or create your own designs. You are limited only by your imagination!

New Year's Confetti Twist

The Dough
1	oz compressed yeast or
1	tablespoon dry yeast
1/4	cup lukewarm water 100 °F (40 °C)
4	cups bread flour
1/2	cup lukewarm milk 100 °F (40 °C)
1/3	cup sugar
1½	teaspoon salt
1	tablespoon lemon zest
1/4	cup melted butter or margarine
2	eggs, slightly beaten

The Filling
1/4	cup soft butter
1/4	cup all-purpose flour
1/4	cup sugar
1	cup coarsely ground blanched almonds
1/2	teaspoon almond extract or

1	teaspoon lemon zest
1/2	cup finely chopped red maraschino cherries
1/2	cup finely chopped green maraschino cherries

The Glaze

1	cup powdered sugar
1	teaspoon vanilla extract
2-3	tablespoons water or milk

Dissolve the yeast in the lukewarm water with 2 tablespoons flour. Blend, cover, and let it rise. Put the flour in a large mixing bowl and make a well in the center. Pour in the yeast and the remaining dough ingredients. Gradually take the flour from the sides and mix with the liquid. Turn the dough out onto a well-floured work top and knead 5-10 minutes, until smooth and elastic. Add flour as needed until no longer sticky. Place the dough in a buttered bowl, brush the top with butter, cover and let rise for about 2 hours, until doubled in bulk.

Prepare the filling: Cream the butter with the flour and sugar. Add the almond extract, or the lemon zest, and the almonds. Combine with your fingers into a loose crumbly mixture, and refrigerate. Punch down the dough and place on a well-floured worktop. Roll out into a rectangle 10x24 inches (25x60 cm). Crumble the filling, and sprinkle over the dough. Sprinkle the red and green chopped cherries on top. Then roll dough up jelly-roll fashion, starting with a long edge. Wet the outer edge to seal. With a sharp floured knife, cut roll in half lengthwise and carefully turn halves so that the cut sides face up. Loosely twist both ropes of dough around each other, keeping cut sides up so filling is visible. Generously butter a round 16-inch (40-cm) baking pan and carefully transfer the roll, shaping it into a circle. Wet the ends and pinch together firmly to seal. If you wish, wrap a single coin in foil and insert it into the dough so it is concealed. According to a tradition in many countries, the one who finds the coin when the bread is cut will have good fortune in the New Year. Cover the wreath with a cloth and let rise in a warm humid place, until doubled in bulk. Bake in a 400°F (200°C) oven for about 20 minutes, until lightly brown. Remove from oven and cool on a rack. In a small bowl, blend the glaze ingredients, gradually adding the water until the desired consistency is reached. Dribble the glaze with a spoon, following the cut edges of the wreath.

Preparation time 3 hours and 30 minutes

HAPPY BIRTHDAY, GRANDMA

MENU

Crudités and Dips

Vol-au-Vent à la Reine

Roast Capon with Onions

Mixed Vegetable Salad

Garlic Dinner Rolls

Bonnet de Nuit or
Chocolate Cheesecake
Watermelon Basket

Melisanthi, Porto Carras or Kallisti, Santorini
Greek White Wine

Crudités and Dips Appetizer

Pasta di Oliva

2²/₃ cups chopped black olive
3 tablespoons corn oil
1 tablespoon vinegar
1 small clove of garlic

Blend the ingredients in a food processor for a few seconds, until smooth and uniform.

Parsley Dip

1 cup finely chopped parsley
3 green onions, finely chopped
2 tablespoons lemon juice
salt and pepper, to taste
10 drops Tabasco sauce
2-3 anchovies, mashed (optional)
2 oz (60 gr) cream cheese
1 tablespoon soft butter

Process the parsley, onion, lemon juice, Tabasco, and

anchovies (if used) in a blender. Add the cream cheese and butter, and blend until smooth. Adjust the seasonings. Cut the tops off a yellow and a green bell pepper, and remove seeds. Fill with the dips and place on a platter, surrounded by sliced or whole fresh vegetables. Put two "handles" cut from pimento or red bell pepper on the pepper-cups so they look like little baskets. Serve the crudités and dippers with crackers and bread sticks.

Preparation time 45 minutes

Vol-au-Vent à la Reine

8 large vol-au-vent pastries

The Filling

1 lb (500 gr) chicken (chicken, breast, wings, and neck)
1/3 cup butter
2 tablespoons flour
1/3 cup cream
2 egg yolks
7 oz (200 gr) small mushrooms, sliced
1/4 cup dry white wine
2 tablespoons finely chopped parsley
salt and pepper
2 tablespoons grated Parmesan or kefalotiri cheese
2 tablespoons grated soft Swiss cheese

In a large pan, place the chicken with 3 cups water, salt, and white pepper. Slowly bring to a boil, over medium heat and skim off the scum. Cover and simmer, until tender. Remove from the stock with a slotted spoon and discard the wings and neck. Debone the remaining chicken, and chop into small pieces. Continue simmering the stock until reduced to ³/₄ cup. Heat 2 tablespoons butter in a saucepan and saute the flour for 1 minute. Stirring vigorously, add the reduced chicken stock and the cream. Simmer until thick. Cool briefly, then fold in the egg yolks one at a time, continuously stirring , until the velouté sauce is smooth and uniform. Melt the rest of the butter in a skillet, and saute the mushrooms until wilted. Add the wine and stir for a few minutes until most of it evaporates. Add the finely chopped chicken, parsley, cheeses, salt, and white pepper. Gently fold the mixture into the velouté sauce and stir over low heat, until heated through. Fill each vol-au-vent with 2-3 tablespoons of the filling. Bake briefly in a 400 °F (200 °C) oven until heated through and serve. Serve the rest of the sauce, separately, in a gravy boat. Alternatively: Substitute shrimp, lobster, crab, or salmon, for the chicken and blanched, chopped asparagus for the mushrooms. For the velouté sauce, use the seafood stock in place of the chicken stock.

Preparation time 1 hour

Vol-au-Vent Puff Pastries

1½   lbs (700 gr) frozen puff pastry (3 large sheets)
1   egg yolk, beaten with
1   teaspoon water

You can buy ready-made vol-au-vents, saving yourself much time and trouble. You can, however, make them at home.

Spread a sheet of puff pastry on a well-floured worktop and cut in half. Roll each half into a square sheet, 12x12 inches (30x30 cm). With a cookie cutter, cut out six 2-inch (5-cm) circles, 2 inches (5 cm) apart, and 1 inch (2.5 cm) from the sides of the first sheet. Brush lightly with water and place the second sheet on top. Turn over. Using a 3-inch (7-cm) cutter, cut 6 larger circles through both layers of pastry, with the 6 holes in the center of each. Carefully remove the two-layer circles of pastry and arrange on an ungreased baking sheet. Roll out two more (same dimensions) puff pastry sheets and place one on top of the other, brushing with a little water in between. With the large and small cutters, cut (through both layers) 6 rings and remove the centers. Brush the tops of the first 6 vol-au-vent bases with water, and place one ring on top of each. If you want even higher vol-au-vents, cut more rings from two more double-layered pastry sheets and place on top of the pastry circles after brushing with water. Refrigerate the vol-au-vents for at least one hour, so they will rise evenly and retain their shape when baked. Brush the rims of the pastries with beaten egg yolk, making sure that no egg touches any other part of the pastry or it will not rise. Carefully prick the inside bottoms with a fork. To ensure even rising, place a metal wire screen 1 inch (3 cm) above the vol-au-vents, resting on metal cookie cutters placed in the 4 corners of the baking sheet. Bake in a 475 °F (250 °C) oven for 5 minutes. Lower the temperature to 340 °F (175 °C) and bake for an additional 10 minutes. Remove the wire screen and continue baking until golden brown. Remove from oven, cool on wire racks. Store in freezer.

Preparation time 2 hours

Roast Capon with Onions

3   lbs (1½ kg) small whole (pickling) onions
1   large capon or rooster (5½ lbs or 2½ kg)
1/2 cup olive oil or margarine
1½   cups white wine
1   minced bay leaf
1   clove garlic
1/2 teaspoon thyme
1   teaspoon herbs of Provence
     salt and pepper, to taste
1   tablespoon flour

Blanch and peel the onions. They can be frozen until used. If the onions are not tender, parboil for 30 minutes, and drain. Heat the oil in a large pan and saute the onions and garlic over medium heat until wilted. Trim, rinse, and drain the capon; season with salt and pepper. Place in a greased ovenproof roasting pan with cover. Remove the onions with a slotted spoon and arrange them around the rooster. Sprinkle with the herbs and pour the oil and wine over the capon and onions. Cover and bake in a 350°F (180°C) oven for 1 hour and 30 minutes, until the capon and onions are tender. Drain off the juices from the roasting pan into a small bowl and skim off 2-3 tablespoons of fat from the surface. Set the remaining juices aside. In a saucepan, heat the fat, stir in the flour and saute for 1-2 minutes, until slightly browned. Add the reserved juices and stir over medium heat until thick. Pour the gravy over the capon. Continue baking uncovered for an additional 30-40 minutes, until the capon is well-browned and the skin is crisp. Baste the capon once or twice with the gravy. Remove the capon from the oven to a platter, and surround with the onions and carrot curls. Garnish the feet of the capon with skirts clipped from the white part of a green onion.

Preparation time 3 hours

Mixed Vegetable Salad

2   cups finely chopped cabbage
1   medium cucumber, finely cubed
1/2 cup diced yellow pepper
1/2 cup diced red pepper
1/2 cup diced green pepper
1/2 cup canned or frozen corn kernels
1/4 cup finely chopped fresh dill
     The Dressing
2   tablespoons wine vinegar
1   tablespoon lemon juice
1/3 cup olive oil
15   drops Tabasco sauce
     pinch of grated garlic
1/2 tablespoon powdered mustard
     salt and pepper, to taste

Chop the vegetables and drain in a colander. Pat dry with paper towels. Drain the corn in a colander and pat dry with paper towels. If using frozen corn, parboil for a few minutes. Store the various vegetables separately in the refrigerator.

Shake the dressing ingredients in a jar and store, tightly sealed, in the refrigerator. When ready to serve, combine the vegetables in a salad bowl, pour on the dressing, and toss. Garnish with a flower cut out from a red pepper and a decoratively cut cucumber.

Preparation time 35 minutes

Garlic Dinner Rolls

1/3   virgin olive oil
5   garlic cloves
4½   cups bread flour
1   tablespoon dry yeast
1   tablespoon sugar
1½   teaspoon salt
1   egg, separated
1   cup lukewarm water 100°F (40°C)
      white and black sesame seeds

Heat the oil in a small non-stick frying pan, and saute the garlic for 2 minutes, until soft and lightly browned. Remove

Chocolate Cheesecake

The Base
1¼ cups crushed vanilla cookies or Graham crackers
1/3 cup melted unsalted butter

The Filling
7 oz (200 gr) melted semi-sweet baking chocolate
1 egg, separated
1/4 cup sugar
7 oz (200 gr) cream cheese
1 teaspoon vanilla extract
1/2 cup whipped cream

Combine cookie crumbs with the melted butter and rub them between your fingers. Butter a 9-inch (22-cm) pie dish with removable bottom and evenly pat the crumb mixture into the bottom and sides. Bake in a 400°F (200°C) oven for 8 minutes, and cool. Melt the chocolate in a saucepan and set aside to cool. Beat the egg white with the sugar to a soft meringue and set aside. Beat the cream cheese, egg yolk, and vanilla in a separate bowl. Fold in ¹/₂ cup whipped cream, the cooled melted chocolate, and the meringue, taking care not to deflate. Empty the filling into the prepared pie crust. Refrigerate until set. Garnish the cheesecake with whipped cream rosettes, and lacy chocolate triangles. To make the lacy chocolate triangles, first draw on sheets of waxpaper. Using a pastry bag fitted with a fine plain tip, apply melted chocolate following the sketched designs. Refrigerate to harden the chocolate. Carefully pull off the waxed paper. Set them upright in the whipped cream. Keep the cheese cake refrigerated until ready to use.

Preparation time 1 hour

the garlic and mash it. Set the frying oil aside. Combine the flour, yeast, sugar and salt in the bowl of a mixer fitted with a dough hook. Mix 2 tablespoons of the reserved oil into the lukewarm water. Add to the flour with the egg white and mashed garlic. Mix the dough at high speed until it gathers around the hook. Continue kneading at low speed for 5 minutes. Turn out on a floured worktop and knead with your hands, gradually adding the remaining oil until it has been absorbed into the dough. Cover and let rise in a warm humid place until doubled in bulk. Punch down and roll out on a lightly floured surface into a rectangular sheet, ¹/₂ inch (1 cm) thick. Starting from a narrow edge, cut strips, ¹/₂ inch (1.5 cm) wide. Lightly roll to lengthen and make the strips round. Tie into knots and press the ends underneath. Arrange the rolls, spaced well apart, on a baking sheet lined with non-stick baking paper. Cover with a cloth, and let rise in a warm humid place until doubled in bulk. Brush the tops with egg yolk beaten with 1 teaspoon water. Sprinkle half the rolls with white, half with black sesame seeds. Bake in a 400°F (200°C) oven for about 15 minutes. Remove from oven and cool before freezing

Preparation time 2 hours and 30 minutes

Bonnet de Nuit

3   chocolate sponge layers
The Filling
2   cups raspberries, blackberries, or gooseberries
1½   tablespoons cornstarch
1/2   cup sugar
1   tablespoon brandy
4   cups 1 lb (450 gr) whipped cream
The Almond Paste
3½   cups finely ground blanched almonds
2½   cups powdered sugar
1   tablespoon lemon juice
1   teaspoon vanilla
2   egg whites, lightly beaten
The Glaze
1½   cups powdered sugar
1   tablespoon lemon juice
1   teaspoon glycerine
1-2   tablespoons water

Prepare the sponge according to the recipe for "Chocolate Mousse Cake" (page 138). Bake in three 9-inch (23-cm) round cake pans.

Prepare the blackberry filling: Place half the berries in a small saucepan with the sugar and cornstarch. Simmer, stirring with a wooden spoon, until thick and clear. Remove from heat and stir in the brandy. Allow to cool and carefully stir in the remaining berries. Center one sponge layer on a round plate, 2 inches larger than the diameter of the cake. Spread half the berry filling on the sponge and half the whipped cream on top. Cover with the second layer. Spread with the rest of the berry filling, and the remaining whipped cream. Cover with the third sponge layer. Refrigerate to set.

Prepare the almond paste: Combine all the ingredients, except for the beaten egg whites, in a bowl. Add just enough egg white to make a moderately thick dough and knead. Transfer the almond paste to a worktop sprinkled with powdered sugar and knead it lightly, until smooth. Divide in half. Roll out half the almond paste into a round sheet, 1.8-inch (0.3-cm) thick, large enough to cover the top and sides of the cake. Roll the sheet around the rolling pin to lift and place onto the cake. Be sure the top and sides are completely covered; then trim the excess with a knife. Roll out the other half of the almond paste into a long thin sheet. Using a scalloped pastry roller, cut strips, 2 inches (5 cm) wide. (Remember to set aside some extra almond paste to color for the ribbon on the bonnet). Carefully ruffle the almond paste strips on one side, making semi-circular frills. Arrange these around the bottom of the cake resting on the edge of the plate.

Prepare the glaze: mix all the ingredients in a bowl, adding enough water to make the glaze rather fluid. Brush the entire surface and sides of the cake with the glaze. Refrigerate until the glaze sets. Decorate the bottom of the cake with small rectangular pieces of pink-dyed almond paste, to resemble a pink ribbon passing in and out of the bonnet.Pipe a bit of green icing on either side of the pink "ribbons". Place a ribbon bow of pink almond paste at one side of the cake. Don't forget to write "Happy Birthday Grandma!" with pink icing on top.

Preparation time depends on your skill and dexterity

Organizing Grandmother's Birthday Party

Celebrate Grandmother's birthday with a recipe from by-gone days, "Roast Capon in Wine". The crudités appetizer and the vol-au-vents provide a light introduction to this hearty dish. Choose a good white wine such as Greek "Melissanthi" from Porto Carras or "Kallisti" from Santorini to accompany both courses.

❀ *Each recipe serves 6 persons.*

❀ *Well in advance, prepare the vol-au-vents,without filling them, the onions for the capon, and the bread rolls. Store in the freezer.*

❀ *Two days in advance, make the Bonnet de Nuit and the chocolate cheese cake. Keep refrigerated.*

❀ *The morning before, prepare pasta di oliva and parsley dip. Wash the vegetables.*

❀ *The evening before, make the filling for the vol-au-vents and the carrot rolls.*

❀ *In the morning, cut the various vegetables for the salad, and refrigerate. Prepare the watermelon fruit basket. Remove the pre-prepared foods from the freezer.*

❀ *During the day, roast the capon with the onions and set the table.*

Watermelon Basket

Select a large, perfect watermelon. Cut it as shown in the picture, creating a basket. Score verticle and horizontal lines into the surface with a chisel, so that it resembles a basket. Hollow out the inside, and fill with various seasonal fruits, washed and patted dry.

USEFUL TIPS

❀ **To keep fresh mushrooms white:** *Cut a thin slice off the bottom of each stem. Wash the mushrooms well and place in a pan. Sprinkle with salt, white pepper, a pat of butter, and 1 tablespoon lemon juice. Add ¼ of a cup water, cover the pan and bring just to the boiling point over high heat. The mushrooms will release most of their juice. Remove from heat and set aside. Just before using, drain the mushrooms.*

❀ **To clarify stock:** *Follow the procedure described in "Vegetable Consommé" recipe, (page 11).*

❀ **To prepare an avocado:** *Cut in half lengthwise with a knife. Separate by twisting the two halves in opposite directions. Insert the point of a very sharp knife into the seed*

and gently twist back and forth to pull it free. Place the cut side down on a wooden cutting board, and peel. Slice with a sharp knife and immediately sprinkle with lemon juice to prevent discoloration. Avocados are eaten only when raw. They turn bitter when cooked.

❀ **To bake bread with a crisp hard crust:** *Spray it with water 3-4 times during the first 10 minutes of baking.*

❀ **To make lightly buttered croutons:** *Cube the bread and bake in a 300°F (150°C) oven until toasted. Melt 2-3 tablespoons of butter, margarine, or oil in a saucepan and toss the croutons in it while they are still hot until lightly buttered on all sides.*

❀ **To thicken a sauce containing butter that has curdled:** *Immediately remove from heat. Add an ice cube and stir vigorously. If this does not work, put a tablespoon of cold water in a small pot and slowly pour in the curdled sauce drop by drop, stirring continuously. If this is unsuccessful, lightly beat an egg yolk with one tablespoon water in a double boiler or in a small pan over very low heat. Pour in the sauce, drop by drop, stirring continuously until smooth.*

Valentine's Dinner

Open the napkin flat. Turn down the top edge to the center, and fold up the bottom edge overlapping the top by 1.5 inch (4 cm).

Accordion-pleat the folded napkin along the width.

Holding the pleats together at the bottom, pull out the free edges inside the pleats of the bottom section.

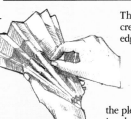

Then pull down and crease the upper folded edges between

the pleats. Tie the pleats in place at the bottom with a red ribbon.

Evening by the Fire

Open the napkin flat, fold in quarters and then diagonally across into a triangle.

Fold the right and left corners of the triangle down, with the edges meeting in the center.

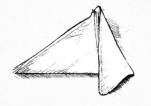

Fold the extending corners under (to the back).

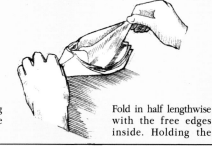

Fold in half lengthwise with the free edges inside. Holding the

folded edges together on the left, pull out the four free corners of the napkin on the right, one by one, so they stand upright.

Carnival Buffet

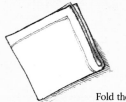

Fold the napkin in quarters.

Fold the first corner back so the tip meets the folded corner opposite, first creasing the cuff across the middle.

Fold the right and left corners to the back, forming a pocket to hold the individual flatware settings

Reunion Dinner

Fold the napkin in quarters. Turn in the folded corner, pointing towards the opposite corner.

Starting at the folded corner, accordion-pleat diagonally.

Place the folded napkin upright in a glass, and open out the four corners.

Easter with the Family

Open out paper napkins. Gather in the middle and stuff into the wine glasses.

Mother's Day Menu

Fold the napkin in half and accordion-pleat crosswise, leaving a 6 inch (15 cm) space uncreased at the end.

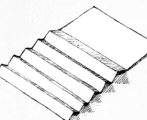

For best results, use a steam iron and spray starch. Always allow ample time for napkin folding.

Fold the pleated side in half. Fold the free corner down to form a triangular base which

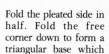

will support the pleats in an upright position. Set the napkin on the table and allow the pleats to fan out.

Congratulations

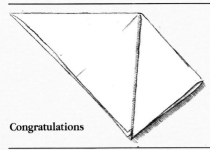

Open the napkin flat and fold it in half into a triangle (base on top, tip pointing down). Bring the two points of the base down to meet at the tip of the triangle. (2 new triangles form a diamond).

Fold these triangles in half by bringing the two free points back up to meet at the folded corner on top. Fold the bottom tip of the original triangle back on

itself extending slightly lower than the bottom edge and crease in place. Tuck the right and left corners into each other at the back. Bring the two free edges down and tuck them into the fold, right and left.

Father's Day Celebration

Open the napkin flat and fold into a triangle, tip pointing down. Fold the top edge (base of triangle) down and turn the napkin over with the fold facing down.

Bring the right and left corners down to meet at the tip of the triangle below.

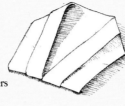

Turn the two sides under and crease to form the "shoulders" and turn all edges at the bottom under and crease. Make small bow ties from dark blue velvet ribbon and place one on each "evening jacket".

Supper by the Seaside

Open the napkin flat and fold in half lengthwise, folded edge down. Fold the right side down to form a triangle.

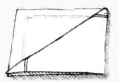

Fold the triangle over onto the left quarter of the folded napkin.

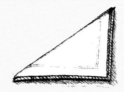

Bring the left corner diagonally down over the folded triangle.

Turn back a 1 inch (2,5 cm) cuff around the bottom edge of the folded napkin.

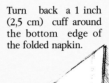

Open the bottom and set the little sailboat on the table.

Engagement Party

Open the napkin flat and accordion-pleat along entire length.

Fold the pleated napkin in the middle.

Pass the folded end through a napkin ring, allowing the pleats to open. If you wish, slip a fresh flower in the ring in keeping with the theme of your party.

Wedding Reception

Open the napkin flat and fold down the top third. Fold the bottom third back with the fold extending slightly lower than the edge of the top third. Fold the 2 corners of

the top third back diagonally forming 2 "wings". Accordion-pleat crosswise along the entire length. Gather the pleats together and hold at the folded end with the wings at the back. With the other hand, pull out the pleats of the lower free edge.

Stuff the gathered pleats at the folded end into a wine glass,

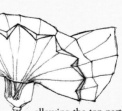

allowing the top part of the napkin to fan out.

Baby's Christening

Fold the napkins according to directions for Valentine's Dinner, leaving the upper edge uncreased.

Moonlight Barbecue

Fold pastel-colored paper napkins into quarters and roll into cones. Coordinate the colors with your table linens, china, and flowers. Arrange the napkins attractively in a basket or crystal bowl.

Silver Anniversary

Open the napkin flat. Fold in opposite sides to meet in the center.

Holding your finger on the center, fold the four corners out diagonally, forming 4 "wings" and crease.

Roll in the right hand side to the center. Pleat the other side of the napkin.

Fold in two with the rolled part in the center. Place in a glass or pass through a napkin ring and allow the pleats to fan open.

 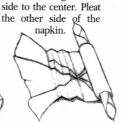 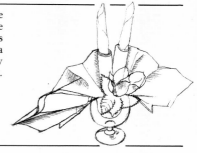

For an Honored Guest

Open the napkin flat and fold in thirds.

Fold the two open ends to meet in the middle.

Fold down both upper corners to meet in the center.

Turn the folded napkin over, with the tip pointing down. Tuck one corner into the other. Turn over and set on the table with the points up. Put a fresh flower in the middle.

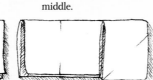 

Golden Anniversary

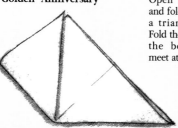

Open the napkin flat and fold diagonally into a triangle, point up. Fold the two sides up so the bottom corners meet at the top.

Fold the bottom (folded) corner up so the point is just below the center and fold it back again so the tip reaches the base.

Bring the right and left corners to the back and tuck into each other. Pull down the free corners from the top, to the right and left and stand upright.

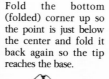 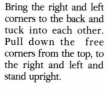 

Nameday Celebration

Open the napkin flat and fold in the four corners in to meet in the center. Fold the four corners in a second time, towards the center.

Turn the napkin over and, once again, fold in the four corners to meet in the center.

Holding down the folded corners in the center with one hand, unfold each of the four

points by pulling up the free edge underneath. Pull up the four original corners of the napkin between each point, forming a "flower" with 8 petals.

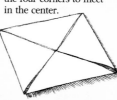 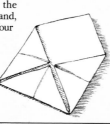 

Festive Holiday Gathering

Open the napkin flat and fold into a triangle. Fold up the base of the triangle once.

Turn the napkin over and roll up from one side to the other, forming a "candle".

Secure by tucking the free end into the fold. Slightly turn the top front point down.

Happy Birthday, Grandma

Fold the napkin in quarters. Roll the top quarter towards the center. Likewise roll the second edge and slip under the first roll.

Continue, rolling the third edge under the second roll, and the fourth under the third.

Roll the folded corner opposite towards the center and, if you wish, secure the edge under the first roll in the center.

GARNISHES AND DECORATIONS

Carrot Curls: With a vegetable peeler, cut thin layers from the length of a thick carrot. Roll up and secure with toothpicks. Put in a bowl of cold water and chill overnight in the refrigerator to stiffen. Remove the toothpicks before using.

Cucumber Garnishes: With a sharp knife, divide a small cucumber in half lengthwise. Put one piece on a cutting board with the cut side down. At a sharp angle, cut one side off. Make four diagonal cuts parallel to the first, 1/8 inch (3 mm) apart, leaving the strips attached at one end. Make a fifth cut and remove the rest of the cucumber. Tuck every other strip inside to make the attractive garnish in the photograph.

Red Pepper Flowers: Stick a sharp knife in the center of a fresh long pointed red pepper. Cut a deep zigzag pattern around the pepper to form 5 petals. Twist the top of the pepper to separate it from the bottom. Remove the seeds, if desired, (or leave them if they are fresh enough). Put the pepper flowers in cold water so the petals open. Use this pretty red flower to garnish a salad or platter.

Decorative Mushroom: Cut and remove thin wedges from around the circumference of a large white mushroom. Put a sprig of fresh dill in each opening.

Onion Crysanthemums: Use large fresh green onions with thick bulbs to make "crysanthemums". Wash and peel

the onions. With a sharp knife make slashes around the onions from a point just below the top to the base, cutting through to the center. First, put them in a bowl of hot water to reduce the odor. Then put them in a bowl of cold water and chill so they will open. You can tint the onion flowers by putting food coloring in the water to make a very colorful garnish for salads. You can also separate the layers of onion and put a radish rosette in the center as pictured on page 69.

Cucumber Baskets: Remove tip from an unpeeled cucumber and cut in 2-inch (5-cm) lengths. Slice a bit off one side and set the cucumber down on this base. In the center, make two parallel slashes 1/4 inch (5 mm) apart half-way down. Then make two perpendicular cuts to the right and left of the parallel slashes and remove these halves. Carefully scrape out the flesh under the "handle". Using small cookie-cutters, make flower shapes from thin slices of carrot and place them onto the baskets.

Decorative Cucumber Flower-Pots: Cut off the end of a thick cucumber. With a sharp knife, make deep zigzag cuts around the circumference of the cucumber at the height of 2 1/2 inches (6 cm), inserting the knife through to the center. Twist the two parts to separate. Scoop out the seeds with a spoon. Separate the peel from the flesh, making a second series of "petals". Put the cucumbers in cold water and refrigerate for several hours so the petals separate and curl back. Stick carrot flowers or tomato peel rosettes and parsley leaves in the centers with toothpicks.

Christmas Candle in Ice: You can easily create this spectacular crystal ice

bowl candle holder: Fill a metal bowl 8 inches (20 cm) wide and 7 inches (18 cm) high with water. Place in the freezer for 6-8 hours. Turn upside down on a deep plate and when the ice starts to melt, it will fall out. With a saw-tooth knife, cut off the top and empty out the water which has not frozen. If it has completely frozen, try again, this time leaving the bowl in the freezer for a shorter time. Keep the

crystal ice bowl in the freezer until ready to use. Place a short red candle in the bowl and use as a centerpiece on your table or sideboard. Light the candle, turn out the lights and let the dancing beams of reflected light bedazzle your guests! The ice bowl will last about 5 hours inside and 12 hours outside in very cold weather.

Cucumber Chain: Score or scrape thin strips from around an unpeeled cucumber with a peel stripper or the tines of a fork. Cut the cucumber into ¼ inch (7 mm) thick rounds and hollow out the center. Make on slash in each ring and pass one through the other to form a chain as pictured in Potpourri Salad on page 69.

Decorative Lemon Twists: With a special peel stripper, scrape off parallel rows of peel, lengthwise, around the lemon. With a sharp knife, thinly slice the lemon crosswise and slash each one from the edge to the center. Twist the two ends in opposite directions and use to garnish salad or fish platters, as pictured in Dandelion Greens Salad on page 144.

White Radish Cones: Cut thin round slices from a white radish. Roll into cones and secure with a toothpick. Put them in cold water and refrigerate several hours until they stiffen. Remove toothpicks before use, as pictured in

Festive Salad on page 163.

Radish Rosettes: With a small sharp knife, cut 4 or 5 petals symmetrically around a red radish without separating them. Put in cold water and refrigerate so the petals open to form pretty rosettes, like those pictured in Beet Salad on page 153.

Cucumber Gondola: Wash and wipe a cucumber. Cut a thin slice off one side and set the cucumber on this base. Cut a thin slice lengthwise from the top of the cucumber, leaving it attached at one end. Using a wooden souvlaki skewer, stand the slice upright in an S-shape with small fruits or olives in between. Scoop out some of the flesh and fill the "gondola" with fresh fruits or vegetables.

Useful information for the accurate measurement of ingredients

Measuring systems used in cooking vary from country to country. The basic systems in use around the world are the following:
1. Imperial: Used mainly in England and Australia, in this system, dry ingredients are measured in Imperial ounces (oz) and liquid, in fluid ounces (fl.oz).
2. Metric: Used in the European Union (EU), dry ingredients are measured in grams (gr) (1000 gr = 1 kilo) and liquids in cubic centimeters (ml).
3. American: Most ingredients, whether dry or liquid are measured in the standard measuring cup based on a volume of 240 ml. The weight of one cup of different ingredients varies, i.e:

1 cup of ingredient weighs (approx)		oz	gr
Bread crumbs, dry	„	3.5	100
Butter or margarine	„	8	225
Cheese, freshly grated	„	4	115
Chocolate chips	„	6	170
Cocoa	„	4	115
Cream, heavy (35%)	„	8	225
Cream, whipped	„	4.5	125
Flour, all-purpose	„	4.5	125
Honey	„	12	350

Milk, fresh whole	„	8.5	240
Nutmeats, ground or grated	„	5-6	140-170
Olive oil	„	8	225
Rice, uncooked	„	8	225
Sugar, granulated	„	7-8	200-225
Sugar, powdered	„	6	170

Conversion formula: oz to gr, multiply oz by 28.35; gr to oz, multiply gr by .035
Listed below are some approximate equivalents of grated or chopped ingredients frequently used:

1 cup whipping cream	yields	2-2½ c. whipped cream
1 lb fresh crabmeat	„	3 cups
5 large eggs	„	1 cup
8 egg white	„	1 cup
1 large onion	„	1 c. chopped onion
1 small onion	„	1/4 c. chopped onion
1 bunch (8) green onions	„	1 c. chopped
8 oz (500 gr) macaroni	„	4 c. cooked
1 large celery stalk	„	1/2 c sliced or chopped
3 carrots (1/2 lb)	„	1½ c sliced or shredded
1 cup rice	„	3 c. cooked

The recipes in this book are given in (°F) and Celsius (°C). The oven should be preheated to the temperature specified, unless specified otherwise. If you have a convection type oven, temperature should be set 65°F (20°C) degrees less than given. When baking or roasting, food should be placed low in the oven so the surface is in the middle of the oven. Place the pan higher when the surface has to brown quickly.

Measuring equivalents

measures	symbol	metric system	symbol
1 teaspoon	tsp	5 cub.centimeters	ml
1 tablespoon	tbsp	15 cub.centimeters	ml
1 fluid ounce	fl.oz	30 cub.centimeters	ml
1 cup	c	0,24 litres	l
1 pint	pt	0,47 litres	l
1 quart	qt	0,95 litres	l
1 ounce	oz	28 grams	gr
1 pound	lb	0,45 kilogram	kg

Oven temperature chart

	electric		gas range
	°F	°C	regulator
very slow oven	225	110	1/4
	250	120	1/2
slow	275	140	1
	300	150	2
moderately hot	325	160	3
	350	180	4
	375	190	5
hot	400	200	6
	425	220	7
very hot	450	230	8
	475	250	9

GLOSSARY

Avgolemono: An egg and lemon sauce made with fresh lemon juice and eggs beaten into hot broth.

Almond Paste: A confection made from ground almonds, sugar and egg white. Sometimes called marzipan or marchpane. Ready-made marzipan is also available commercially.

Aspic: A gelatin mold of reduced and clarified meat or fish stock or vegetable consommé.

Blanch: To immerse food quickly in boiling water to loosen tough outer coverings remove, or strong flavors. Blanching helps preserve vitamins and partially cooks or softens food before further use.

Brik: Red fish roe; a type of caviar.

Brioche: A light, sweet richly flavored French bread, usually made into individual rolls with a characteristic "top knot".

Capon: A neutered male chicken which is prized for its succulent white breast meat.

Caul: A thin membrane marbled with fat which encases the entrails of lamb or kid. It is usually cut into pieces and stuffed with minced meats and fried, broiled or baked.

Clarify: To clarify butter, melt over low heat, skim off the pure fat and discard the milky residue. To clarify broth, see recipe for "Vegetable Consommé" (page, 11)

Crudités: Fresh vegetables cut into bite-size pieces or sticks to accompany dips and sauces.

Crystallized Fruits: Have been cooked in a heavy sugar syrup and then dried. When chopped, they can be mixed in fillings, cake batters or sweet bread doughs. Whole, they are used to garnish cakes and tarts. Sometimes referred to as glazed or candied fruit.

Farfalle: Bow-knot shaped pasta.

Feta Cheese: A soft white cheese made in Greece from the milk of goats or sheep which is ripened in brine.

Fold: To mix food gently from the bottom of the bowl to the top, in an under-over motion that distributes ingredients without breaking down air-bubbles in whipped egg whites or cream.

Fondant: When a sugar syrup is cooked to the soft-ball stage, cooled and then worked continuously, tiny sugar crystals form in it and the syrup gradually becomes a firm, snowy-white paste. This paste is known as fondant.

Gruyère: A creamy Swiss-type of cheese, similar to Emmentaler, but moister with a sharper flavor.

Herbs of Provence: A mixture of Mediterranean herbs including rosemary, thyme, oregano, savory, marjoram, and basil.

Julienned: Vegetables or other foods cut into matchstick-sized pieces of the same length.

Kasseri Cheese: A semi-hard pale yellow Greek cheese of at least 80% sheep's milk and goat milk. Firmer and milder tasting than feta cheese, it melts well and can be substituted for mozzarella cheese.

Kefalotiri: A Greek goatmilk cheese similar to Parmesan, used for grating. Sometimes soft and mild, it becomes hard and sharp with aging.

Knead: To fold, press and stretch dough or any mixture, until it becomes smooth and elastic.

Ladyfingers: Oblong-shaped sponge wafers or biscuits used for making refrigerator desserts. They are usually dipped in milk or liqueur before being used. In France they are called "Savoyard".

Mascarpone Cheese: A soft, white double-cream cheese from Italy.

Mousse: A light airy dish usually made with whipped cream or eggs. Sometimes cooked in a mold, or made with gelatin and served cold as for Bavarian.

Offal: Meats (entrails) found inside the carcass of an animal, such as liver, heat, lungs, spleen, kidneys, sweet breads, and the intestines.

Pâté: Pureed cooked meat, seafood, or vegetables made into a paste, usually served as an appetizer.

Phyllo: Very thin pastry sheets for pites and Anatolian-type desserts such as baklava. Sometimes called strudel leaves, phyllo is now widely available in grocery stores.

Poach: To cook food wrapped in paper or covered in a container over steam or a simmering liquid.

Puree: To force soft cooked food through a strainer or blend in a food processor until a smooth uniform paste is formed.

Purslane: Shiny wide-leaved greens with a slightly bitter taste, usually eaten raw in salads or used as garnish; use cress as a substitute.

Reduce: To cook a liquid or broth gently until the water is evaporated and thickens into a sauce.

Risotto: A classic Italian dish in which rice is cooked with chopped vegetables, cooked meats and topped with Parmesan cheese.

Rocket: A salad green popular for its slightly bitter taste and bright green color in Europe. Sometimes called arugula.

Saute: To fry lightly and quickly, stirring frequently in a small amount of fat or oil over high heat. This process forms an outer crust, sealing in the juices and keeping food from drying out.

Simmer: To cook slowly over slow heat.

Timbale: Food cooked, by steaming or baking, in a drum-shaped mold.

Torte: Recipes in which the flour is replaced by crumbs or finely ground nuts to make a base for a sweet are called tortes, not cakes. They are usually made in a springform pan with removable sides.

Vol-au-Vents: Patty shells made with French-type puff pastry. Usually filled with creamed food or fresh fruits and cream.

Zest: Grating from the colorful outer coating of lemons, oranges and other citrus fruits used to flavor sauces, soups, stuffings, baked goods and desserts.

INDEX